Fighting for Darla

CHALLENGES FOR

FAMILY CARE AND

PROFESSIONAL

RESPONSIBILITY

The Case Study of a

Pregnant Adolescent

with Autism

Fighting for Darla

for

Darla

CHALLENGES FOR

FAMILY CARE AND

PROFESSIONAL

RESPONSIBILITY

The Case Study of a

Pregnant Adolescent

with Autism

Ellen A. Brantlinger

Susan M. Klein

Samuel L. Guskin

Teachers College
Columbia University
New York and London

Published by Teachers College Press, 1234 Amsterdam Avenue
New York, NY 10027

Library of Congress Cataloging-in-Publication Data

Brantlinger, Ellen A.
   Fighting for Darla : challenges for family care and professional
responsibility : the case study of a pregnant adolescent with autism
/ Ellen A. Brantlinger, Susan M. Klein, Samuel L. Guskin.
     p.   cm.
   Includes bibliographical references.
   ISBN 0-8077-3357-1. — ISBN 0-8077-3291-5 (pbk.)
   1. Teenage pregnancy—Case studies. 2. Social work with the
mentally handicapped—Case studies. 3. Autistic youth—Case
studies. 4. Family social work—Case studies. I. Klein, Susan M.
II. Guskin, Samuel Louis, 1932–   . III. Title.
RC570.2.B73   1994
362.3'8—dc20   94-15317

ISBN 0-8077-3357-1
ISBN 0-8077-3356-3 (pbk)

Printed on acid-free paper

Manufactured in the United States of America

98 97 96 95 94   8 7 6 5 4 3 2 1

Contents

Foreword

The authors of *Fighting for Darla* are dedicated educators and researchers who have devoted themselves to preparing future generations of educators and other human service professionals to serve children and adults with disabilities as well as their families. Their teaching and research have always included direct service to children and families because these educators know that the college and graduate school classroom cannot be separate from the real world. In telling the story of Darla, fifteen, autistic, and pregnant, the authors have documented a contemporary tragedy to attempt an understanding of the people and events as they unfold.

Darla is a young woman with autism; she is also mentally retarded. She is a young woman with significant disabilities, living in a world in which issues of women's rights, reproductive rights, and disability rights are hotly debated. It is unlikely that Darla is aware of these debates. We are not even sure that Darla's family pays attention to the issues. In fact, the debates do not even take into consideration a woman like Darla.

Darla's story pushed the limits of many caring individuals. It is impressive that so many resisted the temptation to ignore Darla and her family and refer them as far away as possible—to help them "fall through the cracks" of humane community services.

Darla forces us to question our assumptions and beliefs about our fellow humans. As educated professionals, we expect to be able to do our work, to be helping people in the ways we are accustomed. Darla reminds us that the real world is complicated and never easy; she forces us to struggle with our own sense of helplessness and despair when the real world does not live up to our expectations. Although she has no language we can understand, Darla teaches us. *Fighting for Darla* presents a kind of projective test that confronts us with real life facts—people with disabilities do have sexual relationships and sometimes they are more vulnerable than others to sexual abuse. In a more perfect world Darla would not have become pregnant. However, we must remember that Darla's story is her own as well as the story of the people who became involved in her life. It is not the story of people with disabilities who become parents with fulfillment and joy.

Congratulations to the authors and the publisher of this book. Because Darla's story is not a research report and as a case study it is unorthodox, it was difficult to find a publishing niche for it. We are fortunate that the authors took the risk of sharing their own struggles and uncertainties and brought forth this difficult narrative. They have allowed us to observe the inner struggles of so many individuals in order that we may be less fearful of observing ourselves and become more willing to learn difficult lessons together.

Stanley D. Klein, Ph.D.
Editor in Chief, *Exceptional Parent*
Professor of Psychology, New England College of Optometry

Acknowledgments

First, our respect and gratitude go to "Darla" and, above all, her parents, "Carol and James Helm." Mr. and Mrs. Helm were interviewed or observed alone and together on several occasions. Although they were concerned about family privacy, they also understood the motives of the researchers in trying to present a full picture of Darla's situation. They were open not only to being interviewed, but also to giving their permission for others to share information and perceptions about Darla, her family, and the events of her pregnancy with the researchers. Their understanding and cooperation are very much appreciated by the authors.

Our thanks and admiration are extended to all the other individuals who participated in our study, who, with rare exception, willingly and kindly gave their time and showed so much concern and interest in improving the quality of life for Darla. We are particularly grateful because we recognize that Darla's situation posed potential legal ramifications beyond their control, and, in fact, several of the professionals felt personally threatened and vulnerable in expressing their feelings or in sharing information with the authors. Nevertheless, perhaps because of their genuine interest in Darla and her family, the individuals interviewed seemed to talk freely, and generally volunteered much more information than we had requested.

We are most appreciative of the efforts of Nancy Dalrymple and Marci Wheeler, who coordinated our contacts with the study's participants. To our colleagues and friends who read various versions of the manuscript and provided suggestions and encouragement, we are deeply grateful: Nancy Dalrymple, Robert Agranoff, Phyllis Guskin, Stanley Klein, and Marilyn Irwin. We wish to thank Kay Fatch, who labored for many hours over many months to convert and rearrange the original manuscript onto more advanced word processing software so that we could revise and print our manuscript more efficiently. We are grateful to Brian Ellerbeck, Acquisitions Editor at Teachers College Press, who saw value in our unconventional project and provided timely suggestions to facilitate our development of the manuscript for publication. We also appreciate Carol Collins's careful editing of the manuscript, as well as her helpful suggestions for revisions, and Cynthia Fairbanks's production editing. Lastly, we acknowledge the "Clay Center" administration and program staff for enabling this project to proceed and for providing support at various stages of its development.

Fighting for Darla

CHALLENGES FOR

FAMILY CARE AND

PROFESSIONAL

RESPONSIBILITY

The Case Study of a

Pregnant Adolescent

with Autism

CHAPTER 1

Introduction

At 15 years of age, Darla (a pseudonym as are all other names of people and places in this book) was found to be pregnant. Darla has autism, a developmental disability of unknown cause and varied consequences, such as problems in communication, difficulties with social relationships, ritualistic behavior, and, often, mental retardation. Darla has all of these characteristics of autism, and all in the most severe form. At the time her pregnancy was discovered, Darla attended and resided at a school for teenagers with autism. Much to the consternation of everyone around her, Darla's pregnancy was not discovered until the fifth month—too late for early prenatal care and almost too late to consider abortion. Suspicions arose that her pregnancy was the result of incest. Thus a chain of disturbing events was set into motion, as providing care became intertwined with an emotional search for the individual responsible for Darla's pregnancy.

Darla's pregnancy eventually ran full term and her son, Jason, was delivered by Caesarean section. Soon after his birth, Jason was diagnosed with microcephaly, a condition in which the child has an underdeveloped brain that continues to grow more slowly than the average child's brain. At the time of Jason's birth Darla's parents still were undecided about whether they would raise her child, and Jason's diagnosis triggered further doubts. The caregivers involved with the family were concerned that baby Jason would go into a family already under stress—a family that was being torn apart by the search for his paternity. Carol and James Helm, Darla's parents, had shouldered heavy burdens of responsibility in loving, caring for, and fighting for Darla. People wondered if they could endure the strain of raising their grandchild, who was likely to be as severely retarded as his mother.

A pregnant 15-year-old is regrettably not unusual; a pregnant adolescent with autism and mental retardation was something nobody had expected, nobody had any experience with. It upset many professional assumptions, and caused a crisis in Darla's family. Professionals and relatives familiar with people with autism tell of various signs of sexual feeling and sexual drive among them, but a wide inquiry among people with many years' experience work-

1

ing with people with autism elicited no knowledge of pregnancy among them. A search of the literature proved equally unproductive—there was literally nothing written about such a circumstance.

This story is unusual in that it happens to be about the pregnancy of a 15-year-old girl with autism and severe mental retardation. Yet it touches on the experiences of other families—especially families with a member who has a disability. The presence of a child with autism and mental retardation in a family is a challenge. The story of Carol and James, Darla's parents, shows how ordinary people cope, remarkably, with such a challenge. The story also touches on situations that confront professionals as they carry out their work. It shows how they modify their typical procedures to accommodate someone with special needs. The story sheds light on the ways people deal with a violation of their expectations and assumptions.

Although Darla's situation appeared to be unique, it was rife with issues that constantly face people with disabilities and those who care for them, such as the expression of sexuality, ability to parent, abortion of fetuses known to have major impairments, sterilization of individuals who are too cognitively limited to give informed consent, and access to appropriate educational, social, legal, and medical services. In discussing Darla's case, the authors decided that it should be shared and we set about documenting the events surrounding this situation, beginning shortly after the discovery of Darla's pregnancy and continuing through the first year of the infant's life. The information gained during this process, however, includes informants' recall of the past extending as far back as—even prior to—Darla's own birth.

This is Darla's story. Yet it could take shape only by inferring her thoughts and feelings from our observations of her in numerous settings, and by piecing together information garnered from those close to her. Darla is nonverbal. Many voices contribute to this story; Darla's, unfortunately, is the faintest.

In spite of her inability to talk, Darla is an expressive and communicative person. Her moods are evident and she has obvious mood swings. When she is happy she smiles, giggles, and laughs. When she is upset she snarls, moans loudly, or pinches, scratches, and pulls hair. When Darla hurts others, she sometimes smirks. Some people interpret this as a sadistic side of Darla. Others believe it indicates that she knows more than people generally give her credit for. Still others attribute the smirk to Darla's pleasure at her power to provoke an expressive reaction from others. Darla's moods change rapidly and without apparent cause. She can be working contentedly with a puzzle, then abruptly shove her chair back (so that it bangs to the floor) and start to pace. She can seem calm, then suddenly agitated and forlorn.

When Darla is fond of people, she will hug them, lean against them, or sit on their lap—but she does not do these things consistently. Sometimes she does and sometimes she doesn't. She is unpredictable. When she does not like someone, or if a stranger comes near, she almost always will dart away and pace frantically in a distant corner of the room. If someone dares to come too close at this time, Darla will strike out or she will bang her head against the wall with crashing thuds and howling wails. She likes to be alone in her room, but she will hover around a group if she is familiar with the people. She almost never joins in as part of a group, but she likes to accompany groups on outings.

Darla has preferences. She prefers crunchy foods to soft ones. She particularly loves fresh fruits and vegetables; perhaps that is the reason for her smooth complexion. She likes spacious rooms where she can freely pace. She likes to jump on surfaces with some give, and she will belly flop her body on a bed, or even the floor. She likes to assemble small objects such as puzzles or screws and bolts. If she sees a knob, Darla will attempt to loosen it (and has been observed to swallow small objects, such as knobs, and many other inedibles). Darla likes pictures on walls to be straight, counters clean, and dishes in cupboards to be placed in orderly lines. She likes to look out closed windows and crawl out open ones. Sometimes she breaks windows. She loves to shower and be in a tub or pool. She likes to swing, run, and ride in cars.

Darla likes to do things her own way. She backs off if someone tries to teach her something new. She will strike out or fall prone to the floor if pressured to conform. Darla learns best by observing. She does not immediately imitate a model, but it seems she surreptitiously watches someone else perform a task, then, eventually, when nobody is looking, she sometimes will sidle over and do it herself. Occasionally she works diligently on a task for several minutes, but usually she avoids doing any of the activities in a classroom, even though it is assumed she is capable of doing many of them.

We could watch Darla and conjecture about what she was thinking and the motives behind her behaviors, but Darla could not tell us her story in words. Many things about Darla remain unexplained, and many events in her life are unexplainable. Nevertheless, people around Darla find her intriguing; they like to think about her and talk about her. A number of people told us about Darla and her situation. So, in addition to being Darla's story, our book includes the feelings and opinions of people who knew her.

The immediate impetus for documenting the events of Darla's pregnancy was not to write a book. When administrators of the program in which Darla was enrolled learned of her pregnancy, they promptly called on colleagues to interview those responsible for her care. Their motives in making this request were varied. First, they knew staff members were upset about the situation and so they wanted to provide supportive listeners to help them through the difficult times. Second, they wanted the feelings and actions of the staff to be documented; that is, they wanted a "paper trail" of events that occurred during this time in case outsiders—or insiders, for that matter—questioned the handling of the situation. Third, since the pregnancy of an adolescent with autism seemed to be a unique occurrence, it was deemed important to keep track of it.

RESEARCH METHOD

In chronicling the events of Darla's story, we saw ourselves primarily as facilitators of communication and organizers of information. We wanted to convey the variety of points of view that surfaced as we started talking to people familiar with Darla's situation. We tried to limit our interpretations of circumstances and participants' perspectives because we wanted those involved to contribute to this story in their own ways. As our research progressed, we were further convinced that capturing the insecurity, doubt, ambivalency, and conflict—both within and between participants—was particularly important to this story. Often the professional literature, especially "how to" textbooks, implies that a consensus exists regarding meeting needs and delivering services to people with disabilities. On the contrary, our research has led us to the strong conviction that tentativeness, anxiety, and misgivings often surround the actions of those providing care as well as those who receive care.

Participants

Within a few days of the discovery of Darla's pregnancy, interviews were scheduled with the "Clay Center" staff members who had direct contact with Darla or indirect responsibility for her. (In this book, the program in which Darla was enrolled at the time of her pregnancy is referred to as the "Clay Center.") During the time we were interviewing Clay Center personnel, we became aware of reactions to the situation in Darla's home community. We began to entertain thoughts of extending our study to include people outside the Clay Center who were involved with Darla during this eventful time. It was suspected that such professionals as doctors and judges would be too busy to spend much time with us. Contrary to expectations, they talked for long periods of time and volunteered much more personal information than they were asked. The number of participants burgeoned as those interviewed named others who they felt would have knowledge of Darla's situation.

Of course, Darla's parents were central to our understanding of her situation. Initially, we were hesitant to contact "the Helms," in part because we did not want to burden them during this busy and stressful time, but also because we felt they might resent our interest, especially since the sexual abuse aspect of the case was still unresolved. However, just as Janko (1992) found in her study of parents in sensitive situations, Darla's parents readily agreed to be interviewed. They seemed to appreciate the opportunity to express their opinions and talk about their feelings. In fact, they frequently contacted us when there was a new development or when they thought of something else they wanted to discuss. Furthermore, they seemed pleased that we took their situation seriously enough to write a book about it.

Carol and James Helm were interviewed or observed alone and together on several occasions. Not only were they open to being interviewed, but they gave their permission for others to share information about the family and the situation and even volunteered names of people they thought should be interviewed "for the book." Each time we saw them they added others to that list. Although our original intention was to document the immediate events and feelings surrounding the pregnancy, both parents encouraged us to interview the school personnel and medical professionals they had been involved with during earlier years. They wanted us to go back in time and tell the whole story of Darla's life as well as their lives with Darla.

In the end, 52 people were interviewed, 36 of whom were given pseudonyms (see Appendix A). The remaining 16 either are not quoted in the text or, when quoted, are described by role only. In addition to Darla, six other individuals were observed but not interviewed, and 12 individuals appear in the story only as they were referred to by the interviewees; they were neither observed nor interviewed. Participants included community professionals from Darla's home town of "Winthrop," from "Mapleton" (a fairly large city close to Winthrop), from "Clay County" (location of the Clay Center), and from "State Capital," as well as agency personnel from the "Clay Center." These individuals all had some responsibility for Darla's care, either before, during, or after her pregnancy.

Interview Protocol

Before our enterprise became "a study," we conducted a preliminary round of interviews with some Clay staff using a hastily assembled set of questions. Basically, individuals were encouraged to talk about anything of interest to them regarding Darla. Because at that point we saw our mission as primarily therapeutic, those interviewed were especially encouraged to discuss their own reactions to and feelings about the situation. During these initial interviews, certain questions seemed to surface naturally.

When we decided to formally study Darla's situation, we modified questions and firmed up the sequencing of items (see Appendix B). As might be noted, the protocol consists of open-ended, generic questions likely to elicit responses that reveal participants' own interpretations of the circumstances of Darla's pregnancy (see Glaser & Strauss, 1965, 1967). We also continued to use this protocol in a flexible manner. Because of a desire to turn the interview agenda over to participants as much as possible, we followed their "trains of thought" and were patient when they went off on tangents. The interviewees were continually encouraged to relate this situation to their own experiences and values.

Procedures

Individuals usually were interviewed in their homes or places of employment. Interviews lasted a minimum of an hour and many went on for several hours. The informants who had the most contact with Darla or her family were interviewed on numerous occasions over an extended period of time. Although the sessions were audiotaped, the interviewers took notes while the respondents talked, an approach that allowed us to save the time of transcribing complete interviews. Audiotapes were transcribed when a respondent spoke too quickly for note taking, and were referred to when notes lacked clarity, or when a verbatim quote from the narratives was desired. Data from the interviews that seemed inconsistent or unclear were presented to respondents in order to clarify misconceptions or to elicit more detail about certain aspects of the story.

Our documentation process depended mainly on personal interviews, but we tapped a number of sources in writing this book. An abundance of information was gleaned from perusing staff journals, the minutes of Clay Center staff meetings and case conferences, logs of telephone conversations, and an array of written materials about Darla, including case history information, letters, memoranda, reports, and daily logs of Darla's behaviors at the Clay Center. In addition to interviews and document inspection, observations were made of Darla, her baby, and various members of her family as they interacted with each other at the Clay Center, in the courtroom, in the hospital, and in their home. In other words, we collected "thick data" (Geertz, 1973).

MODELS FOR OUR RESEARCH

Darla's story falls through the cracks of standard types of studies and research presentations. It perhaps comes closest to being a case study—not of a person or a setting, but of a situation. The situation involved a number of individuals, few of whom were personally acquainted with each other, but all of whom were connected through having some responsibility for Darla. Somewhat of a biography, it is pulled away from the single purpose of telling an individual's story by its focus on the positions of others as they cared for Darla.

Although we did not have exact models, other books attempt to portray actual situations of people with disabilities and, at the same time, incorporate the serious unresolved issues they face. Three of the best of these are early post-school, post-institution follow-up studies, including Robert Edgerton's *The Cloak of Competence* (1967); Anne-Marie Henshel's *The Forgotten Ones* (1972); and Janet Mattinson's *Marriage and Mental Handicap* (1971). Later studies that explore everyday life from the perspective of people with disabilities are Robert Bogdan and Steven Taylor's *Inside Out: The Social Meaning of Mental Retardation* (1982); Robert and Martha Perske's *Circle of Friends* (1988); and Karen Schwier's *Speakeasy* (1990). In most cases, participants in these studies had sufficient verbal fluency to tell their stories to recorders.

Perhaps most similar to our book because of its inclusion of multiple views is John Gleason's (1989) ethnographic study of a few institutionalized severely disabled individuals and their care providers. Instead of being broadly issue-oriented, however, Gleason focuses rather exclusively on the intentional and purposeful actions and the unique aspects of the personality of a few individuals diagnosed as severely retarded.

Because of their lack of literacy skills, people with intellectual disabilities have rarely had their stories written from the first-person perspective. A notable exception is *The World of Nigel Hunt: The Diary of a Mongoloid Youth* by Nigel Hunt (1967). On the other hand, first-person narratives are fairly common among parents, particularly among parents who are also professionals in the human services. Greenfield was introspectively open about the ups and downs of parenting a child with disabilities in his *A Child Called Noah* (1965) and then *A Place for Noah* (1978). Helen Featherstone wrote *A Difference in the Family* (1981), detailing the uncertainties of life with her multiply handicapped son from the time the family gradually became aware of the extent of his disability and describing subsequent feelings at various stages of his—and other family members'—development. Sondra Diamond (1993), a psychologist who is severely disabled herself with cerebral palsy, wrote a moving account of her parents', as well as her own, bewildered, ambivalent, and guilt-ridden responses to her physical disability.

In reaction to the ubiquitous focus, in the literature on families with disabled offspring, on problems and deficits, Wickham-Searl (1992) determined to write about successful mothers. Nevertheless, she proceeded to quote mothers' accounts of barriers and frustrations, as well as their own coping skills. Wickham-Searl's work graphically documents a pattern that the four authors have observed in parents of children with disabilities as they gradually give up their crusade to make their children normal. More than acceptance, this phenomenon appears to be an existentialist resolution to the intense, personally consuming search. Parents seem to step back and evaluate their own life's journey as more interesting and enlightened than others' because of their unique child.

UNDERSTANDING OUR PURPOSES AND BIASES

Because this book has three authors, we bring an abundance of purposes and biases to our project. We all have a commitment to helping families raise well-adjusted and independent children—whether those children have disabilities or not. All of us believe that children and adults with autism should be integrated into community life to the fullest extent possible. That means that they should have access to all the public and private community services available to others. We all acknowledge the fact that people with disabilities have sexual feelings and drives and that they should be helped to express their sexuality in a safe and satisfying manner. We certainly believe that professionals should have the best interests of clients and families clearly in mind when interacting with them. We understand that sometimes professionals have to make difficult decisions and take risks to serve them well.

Things happened quickly during the 4 months between the discovery of Darla's pregnancy and her son's birth. While Darla was pregnant, she was desperately in need of caring and informed professional services, and her whole family was in need of support. This time was difficult for everyone, but particularly for Darla's parents. Darla's story highlights caring and supportive individuals, many of whom showed considerable skill and kindness in dealing with Darla and her family at a stressful time. The story also reveals that others were callous and cold. These individuals may have been too overwhelmed with other commitments to take time for Darla. Perhaps they worried—with good reason—that Darla's situation would demand too much of them or would entail personal or professional risks. They may have felt they had insufficient information about people with autism to be of use, or perhaps they held stereotypes that interfered with providing good care. We are aware that there rarely are easy answers in difficult situations. Sometimes what is right for one person causes problems for another. For whatever reason, regardless of Darla's very evident need for services, some professionals avoided involvement. Because many of these same individuals did not share their perspectives with us, their motives had to be gleaned from others' reactions to them. Perhaps the others' reactions were unduly negative. Many of our informants took strong stands, and we facilitated the voicing of those stands in this book. We felt that the conflicts, ambivalencies, and evasions in the situation should be aired—as well as the cooperations, support, and consensus.

We did attempt to be true to the perceptions, opinions, and feelings of all respondents. We listened to family members and professionals as they tried to come to terms with their own ambivalence about unsettling circumstances. Although this is a true story, it might have been constructed as a catalyst for the consideration of a number of silenced issues. Darla's situation was indeed rich with the most controversial challenges to people with disabilities, to families, and to professionals.

The case involves abortion—even second trimester abortion—and abortion of a fetus that, if tested by amniocentesis, would have been found to be impaired. Embedded in the knowledge of prenatal disability is the issue of "wrongful birth"—that the doctors should have informed the parents of the likelihood of disability and should have done the requisite tests to document disability or rule it out (Beauchamp & Childress, 1989; Harris, 1990). The results of those tests would then lead to debates about who decides the fate of the impaired fetus—the parents who think they will raise the child or the government that may end up responsible for (paying for) its care (Jackson, 1990).

Sterilization issues figure prominently on several fronts, including its advisability for minors, for those unable to give informed consent, for those who could not be adequate parents, and for those who cannot understand the meaning of pregnancy and childbirth yet are fully able to become pregnant (Brantlinger, 1992a; Lilford, 1990). It documents the procedures followed, as well as the barriers that were confronted, in obtaining court permission for sterilization. Court approval of sterilization then led to recognition of "conscience statutes"—the legal rights that permit doctors and hospitals to refuse to participate in medical procedures such as abortion or sterilization on moral or ethical grounds (Sloan, 1988).

Darla's case brings up the difficult subject of sexual expression of minors and of individuals with retardation and autism (Ruble & Dalrymple, 1993; Sullivan, 1992). It addresses the disturbing topic of incest. It requires a hard look at "sexual abuse" by asking the reader to evaluate the culpability of a girl who falls into a category that is typically perceived as innocent and vulnerable to sexual victimization. Then it examines official response to the sexual abuse of a minor with disabilities.

Darla's story entails the vulnerability not only of an adolescent with disabilities, but of other family members, and even of professionals as they attempt to serve her needs. Darla's story draws attention to what happens to a family whose energies are overwhelmingly expended on meeting the needs of only one of its members. It graphically illustrates situations in which parents and professionals do not act as "partners" (Brantlinger, 1991a; Wood, 1988). Lastly, the story challenges professional objectivity by exposing personal subjectivity and frailty, as well as describing the constraints that block access to appropriate service delivery (Brantlinger, 1983, 1988a, 1988b, 1991b, 1992b). Instead of reviewing the research findings or theoretical principles related to these issues, this book contextualizes them naturally through the personal narratives of people confronted with implications of the issues.

Darla's story is a vehicle for surveying the resources available to meet the needs of a pregnant adolescent with severe disabilities in a specific geographical location—a story that is demographically unique but likely to be representative of what might be found elsewhere. The story not only explores people's feelings about segregated and inclusive settings for people with severe disabilities, but documents the drawbacks and benefits of these settings. We acknowledge that just as people with disabilities are not a homogeneous group, neither are families with children who have disabilities (Paul, Beckman, & Smith, 1993). We know that this story describes only one family's experiences. On the other hand, there are certain generalized experiences contained within the act of parenting. More particularly, there is a core of commonalities in parenting children with disabilities. The extremity of the sequence of events in Darla's case may be exceptional, but the issues that arise have wide application.

In writing this account of Darla's story, we were committed to making the material as accessible as possible. The events of Darla's story made it clear that a number of different people—family members, school teachers, lawyers, doctors—at various points needed more information about people with autism and about the kind of care appropriate for them and their families. Parent support groups, students of special education, policy planners and evaluators all may possibly find, in the crises that developed in Darla's world, material that stimulates, questions, and challenges their thinking about issues that surface when individuals and families struggle with some of the consequences of developmental disabilities. We hope that our book is useful to families and professionals as they attempt to do their best in their own particular circumstances.

CHAPTER 2

Darla's Family

Winthrop, the county seat of Hudson County, has a population of about 8,000. The center of town is dominated by a large Victorian style red brick courthouse that, to a potential preservationist's delight, seems not to have been tampered with to meet more modern needs or fuel costs. The ceilings are high, stairways expansive, and wainscoting thickly varnished, and the intricately patterned tiled floor would please a quilter. County legal and revenue agencies are still housed in the quarters originally designed for them a century ago. The heavy furniture and paneling in the courtroom reveal the veneration of its architects for the law. Even the people in the courthouse reflect an earlier era. The women put an effort into their grooming and might be described as stylish if their outfits were more current in mode. The judge is formally dressed and has a dignity beyond his years. The lawyers that assemble in the corridors might have stepped off a John Wayne set, giving a western appearance. They wear boot-like shoes with 2-inch heels and pointed toes. Unlike city lawyers, they seem to prefer a macho cowboy to an Ivy League image. Old men in overalls and young men in jeans, jean jackets, and visored caps with the names of beer or fertilizer brands share chewing tobacco as they sit on the benches that line the halls. The people who come and go all greet each other with varying degrees of enthusiasm, from a simple head nod to a warm and prolonged handshake or hug. The pace is slow in Winthrop. Nobody apologizes for being late for appointments.

The businesses that face the courthouse around the square clearly are not thriving. Most have not been renovated or even painted for a number of years. Like many small-town squares, Winthrop has a number of spaces that are temporarily, if not permanently, vacant. There are two coffee shops and five bars on the square, and Winthrop residents can tell you who frequents which one. Radiating in all directions from the square are majestic older homes, most in various states of disrepair and decay. Driving west from the square, one passes about six blocks of tiny, thin-walled cottages before the dwellings change to ranch and split-level style houses, and then the highly visible signs of fast-food chains and discount stores begin to appear on the horizon. The pace is more rapid in this part of town, although the parking lots in the mall are sparsely occupied even here. Winthrop is growing, but not at the same rate as other areas in the state closer to urban centers. New industry in the area is not apparent; farming and coal mining are still the major types of employment.

The Helms' mobile home is situated on the outskirts of Winthrop, about 2 miles west of the town center past the mall and a trailer park with about 30 to 50 trailers. After passing about 10 acres of fields, one can spot the Helms' trailer at the top of the hill. The Helms moved their trailer from the trailer park to this location a few years earlier in order to "have more privacy."

Although there are only two adults in the family, three family cars are parked in front of the trailer (the Helms own a truck, too, which is at James's workshop). A large swing set, homemade and well-built, is on one side of the house, and a garden tilled and ready to plant is on the other. The view from the front steps of the trailer is spectacular. On clear days the clock on the county courthouse is visible. About a half mile down the hill to the west the four-lane highway that connects the state capital (200 miles south) and Mapleton (30 miles north) can be seen. The only house in sight is about 50 feet behind the trailer. Its inhabitant is an elderly single man, with whom the Helms have little to do.

The mobile home was originally a two-bedroom structure, but one of the bedrooms has been divided down the middle to make two narrow, doorless rooms off the living room. Darla's (currently Missy's, while Darla is away at the Clay Center) bedroom is on one side and Jimmy's is on the other. When Darla is home, Missy sleeps on the living room couch. Carol and James's bedroom is on the opposite end of the trailer, separated from the living room by the kitchen and bathroom, which are back to back. The family eats at a stainless steel and formica table in the kitchen. Five at the table would be very crowded. When Darla is at home, she usually eats in her bedroom at a child-sized table.

The trailer has as much furniture as it possibly could hold. The rooms are decorated with school pictures of the children and plants in front of every window (Carol loves plants and gardening). Raw vegetables are Darla's favorite food; in fact, she will choose them over candy. In the summer Carol lets her "raid the garden." Next to the couch in the living room is a 3' by 5' bookcase that contains encyclopedias, a set of science books, various reference books, well-worn children's books, art materials, and games. A home computer is on a desk between the entrances to the bedrooms. Although the carpets and furniture are not new and appear somewhat shabby, the house is clean. Carol apologizes for two boards on the floor at one end of the couch just outside of Darla's bedroom. Darla had a habit of coming out of her room and jumping on that spot, where there used to be some give, until she finally went through the floor. It is difficult to get under the trailer to repair the damage, so the boards may be a permanent fixture in the living room. Carol seems to be proud of her home and mentioned a couple of times that she and James have "done well" for themselves.

CAROL'S STORY

Carol was born in a small town located about 150 miles from her present home. Her only brother, Danny, a year older, has a "muscle condition that affects his legs" and has used a wheelchair all his life. Carol's father was a construction worker, which meant the family moved frequently in order to follow employment, but also because he did not like to stay in one place for long. He died 2 years prior to the interview. Carol remembers him as "rough, but caring." Dot, Carol's mother, was 15 when Carol was born. Dot presently lives about 2 hours away from her daughter, in a neighboring state, close to where Carol was born. Dot visits Carol and her family about once every 2 weeks, or "whenever she is needed." Dot has always been a source of support to Carol, who describes her mother as a strong, quiet, caring person, loving to everyone she cares about, which includes her entire family. When she was growing up Carol felt a strong need to please her mother. She describes herself as similar to her mother in her fervent family attachments. As with Dot, Carol's husband and children come first in her life.

Because of their frequent moves, Carol never completed a school year. Every fall she started in a new school, and when school officials asked to see previous school records, the family would claim they had lost them. By sixth grade her lack of schooling "caught up with her"; Carol was behind and frustrated by the difficulty of the work. Math was hard for her, but she was more anxious about reading and spelling. When she was asked to read out loud, she could not recognize the big words in the sixth-grade text. She failed most of her weekly spelling tests. Carol did not pass sixth grade. By fall they had moved again, so Carol did not bother to enroll in school. At the age of 12 she was 5'3" (her present height) and looked older than her years. Her brother Danny had the same school attendance pattern. Carol's mother empathized with her children's dread of school. She knew they felt humiliated because of what they did not know. She attempted to teach them at home, and Carol claims that the reading skills she does have she learned from her mother. Carol blamed teachers for her decision to quit school. According to Carol, instead of trying to understand why she was behind and helping her learn, teachers got angry at her and made fun of her in front of the class.

Carol manages to conceal her academic inadequacies by a number of inventive strategies: She writes short notes to teachers (e.g., "Jimmy was sick"), and the teachers think that her curt notes are a form of "being cute." They know Carol as a person with a sense of humor. The most difficult time for Carol is when she goes to parties where people are playing some kind of game that involves writing. She then makes up an excuse for not playing. In spite of her lack of academic skills, Carol claims that she never has felt "dumb." She admits that she felt inadequate in school, but claims a "stubborn streak" would not allow others to put her down. In most ways she feels strong and powerful in comparison to others. She is not easy to intimidate.

When she was 16, Carol's family moved to James's home town, which is about 20 miles from Winthrop, just across the state line. Carol met James when she was a carhop in a drive-in restaurant where James and his friends hung out. James, who had just graduated from high school, was about 10 months older than Carol. They married within 2 months of meeting, then moved to Winthrop, following James's parents, his sister, and his brothers.

Carol worked in restaurants and factories after quitting school and occasionally after their marriage, especially at times when work was slow for James and the family needed money. James is a machinist and recently bought his own shop in Winthrop. He has five employees, including his brother Dale. Carol does the bookkeeping and accounts for James. A corner of their bedroom serves as her office. Carol is proud of her ability to do the work and is grateful to James for encouraging her and having confidence in her. Carol claims that James has always respected her and reminded her that she is smart in spite of her lack of literacy skills.

At the time of their marriage, Carol was 17 and James was 18. Darla was born a year later, and James Jr. (Jimmy) arrived 11 months after Darla. It was 9 years before their next child, Missy, was born, at which point Carol had a tubal ligation. Carol turned 34 during Darla's pregnancy.

Memories of Darla's Childhood

Darla was a colicky baby; during the first few months of her life she cried and spit up frequently. Carol, who was breastfeeding Darla, eventually learned that she was eating the wrong kinds of food. When she changed her diet, Darla's irritability and discomfort diminished. After that she was rarely sick. Carol recalled that Darla was precocious in development during her first year, exceeding the charts in almost every area. She walked at 8 months and could say a number of words before she was a year old. Sometime after Jimmy's birth, Darla's behavior began to change. Her attempts to say words decreased and she became more aimlessly active. By the time Darla was 16 months old Carol began to worry that the behavior was not a temporary regression caused by the addition of Jimmy to the family, as she had first surmised, but a serious problem. Jimmy was a good baby and did not demand much attention.

In retrospect, Carol judged her knowledge about child development to be inadequate when her first two children were babies; therefore she did not know how to evaluate Darla's progress. As Jimmy developed, Carol had a chance to observe normal development and was able to recognize Darla's problems.

Carol complained of Darla's high activity level and lack of speech to their pediatrician, Anthony Wilder, when Darla was about 16 months old. Wilder assured her that there was nothing wrong with Darla. By the time she was 2, Darla was speaking only about one word a week. Wilder told Carol that Darla was simply spoiled, that Carol made things too easy for her. He suggested that she deprive Darla of things she wanted so that she would have the incentive to ask for them. Carol followed Wilder's instructions, but the strategy did not increase Darla's speech.

At about this time Carol noticed strange lapses in Darla's attention. Darla would suddenly stop what she was doing and stare, and would not respond to her mother. These lapses in attentiveness were sometimes accompanied by strange body movements. Carol was convinced that her daughter was having seizures, but Dr. Wilder tried, again, to reassure her that there was nothing wrong with Darla. He suggested that Darla's unusual behaviors were a form of temper tantrum used to get attention or something she wanted. The episodes became more intense and lasted longer. There was no doubt in Carol's mind that Darla was having seizures; her main concern was to convince Dr. Wilder. Darla finally had a seizure that lasted long enough for them to get her to the hospital before it was over so that the doctor could observe what was happening. At last, Dr. Wilder confirmed Carol's diagnosis: grand mal seizures. He suggested that Darla probably had been experiencing petit mal seizures previously. He ordered an electroencephalogram (EEG), but later told Carol that the test showed the brain was "normal."

Because of her seizures and hyperactivity, Darla demanded a great deal of attention. Carol felt that she had never neglected Darla; in fact, she thought she had paid just as much attention to her after Jimmy's birth as before. Carol did not feel that Darla's condition was caused by lack of love and attention, but Dr. Wilder suggested that the closeness of Jimmy's birth probably caused Darla's problems. This was one of a series of medical opinions that Carol claims made her feel guilty and inadequate in her maternal role.

The Problem of Diagnosis. The first doctor to label Darla was a psychiatrist in Capital City who examined her when she was about 3 or 4 years old. He stripped the clothes off Darla and had her walk naked down the hall. After asking Carol a few questions, he announced that Darla was retarded. He said he could tell Darla was retarded by the way she walked. Carol had noticed that Darla had a unique walk: There was sort of a hop to it, but Carol thought it was cute. Although she was bothered by the diagnosis, Carol was not convinced that Darla was retarded. As far as Carol was concerned, someone would have to find something wrong with Darla's brain before she would agree to the retardation label.

The Helms were desperately seeking someone who could provide them with a more suitable diagnosis and, more important, get Darla started with a treatment to eliminate her strange behaviors. Besides trying all the local doctors, through the years they heard about more distant experts who might be able to help. One such place was a well-known school for the deaf. Nothing was wrong with her hearing. Another attempt was a hospital in a large city about 400 miles from Winthrop. The Helms moved to the city partly to seek better employment for James, but mostly because the hospital's good reputation offered the promise of help for Darla. By this time Darla was 5. It was there that the Helms first heard the term "autistic-like." However, doctors said that Darla had only some of the symptoms of autism: She did not twirl or spin objects, and she was not fascinated with appliance sounds. Another EEG and complete physical detected nothing physically wrong with Darla. In fact, Darla continued to thrive physically—she was a healthy, robust, attractive little girl.

Since the treatment offered at the hospital was a rather standard preschool program, which did not appear to improve Darla's condition, and James had been unable to find decent employment, after a year the Helms family moved back to Winthrop where they would be closer to family and James could go back to working in his father's machine shop.

After their return to Winthrop, Carol again took Darla to Dr. Wilder, who finally agreed that Darla's worrisome behaviors were not a product of Carol's imagination. However, this return visit to Wilder was their last. Wilder did the unforgivable; he suggested that Carol and James institutionalize Darla, to ease their burden of raising this difficult child. Thereafter, when Darla needed medical care, they took her to their general practitioner, Dr. Edge.

Trying Residential Treatment. Carol wanted Darla to stay at home, but she also wanted the best care for her daughter and again sought professional help. Although Darla was of school age, Carol had no faith that public schools would meet her needs. Carol carried painful memories of her own schooling into her parenting role. When Darla was almost 6 years old, the Helms enrolled her in the Children's Psychiatric Treatment Center in Mapleton, which was about 45 minutes from their home. Dr. Lovell, the director of the center, agreed that Darla was autistic and retarded, but he also diagnosed her as "mainly schizophrenic." Carol recalled Dr. Lovell saying that Darla "hated" them. Her impression was that Lovell attributed Darla's condition to negative parent/child interaction. Because of the presumed family conflict, Lovell would allow the Helms to visit Darla only for 30 minutes once a month. He insisted that more interaction would interfere with treatment.

After Darla had been at the center for a few months and Carol and James had observed no improvement in her condition, they questioned Dr. Lovell. Lovell assured them that Darla was well-behaved at the center, that she talked, and that she was doing first-grade work. Again, he emphasized that the Helms would not see these changes because Darla reverted to her old self in their presence. From the beginning, the Helms had been skeptical about Lovell's diagnosis. Darla had always been affectionate with her family, so Carol found it hard to believe that her condition was caused by hatred of them. Dr. Lovell made claims, but provided no evidence of Darla's supposed progress. Furthermore, they observed Darla to be atypically lethargic and suspected this was due to "too much medication." Most of all, Carol and James missed Darla and wanted their daughter home with them.

When Darla had been at the center about 6 months, the Helms contacted Ken Ingalls, Special Education Director at Winthrop, to talk about the possibility of Darla attending school. (Ingalls recalled this first conversation and described Carol as suffering from "separation anxiety.") In the end, they decided to leave Darla at the Mapleton clinic, with the hope that Lovell's claims about progress were genuine.

Darla had always been a slender—at times even skinny—little girl, but during her months at Mapleton she gained considerable weight. The Helms assumed the weight gain was due to the nature of institutional food. Darla looked bloated, however, rather than fat. In May, after she had been at the Mapleton clinic for 10 months, the Helms finally got permission to bring Darla home for a weekend visit. On their arrival at the clinic, they found her to be bruised in a number of places. Her lips were split and swollen and she had black eyes. She looked as if somebody had hit her face. Instead of going home, they immediately went to the emergency room at the hospital, where Darla was admitted as a patient. Although they assumed that Darla had been beaten, the emergency room doctor told them that the swelling, broken blood vessels, and split skin were all caused by medication. Darla remained in the hospital for over a week until the effects of the medicine subsided.

After their daughter was settled in the hospital, James Helm went to the police and, eventually, to various other agencies in Mapleton. The Helms were convinced that their daughter had been seriously mistreated. The police took no action and the agencies referred them back and forth; none would investigate the Mapleton clinic. Carol and James tried to get the newspaper to cover the story, but their request was refused. Carol concludes that agency, police, and newspaper staff were more willing to accept the professionals' version of events than the parents'.

A determined woman, Carol proudly recalls how she was able to "sneak-ily" obtain the names of other parents whose children were patients at the Mapleton clinic. On contacting them, she found that many had had similar experiences and similar concerns. For many, her call was a welcome one. Eventually this group of parents got the center investigated and closed, although it reopened, supposedly under a different directorship, a short time later. Meanwhile the staff at the center had counter-accused the Helms of abuse of Darla—a case that was dropped for lack of evidence.

Experiences with Public School. After their experience at Mapleton, Carol and James were determined not to let Darla out of their sight. Aware that Darla was now at home, Ken Ingalls contacted the Helms to inform them that Darla had to be enrolled in some educational program or he would be forced to file neglect charges. At 7 years of age, Darla was of mandatory school age. But the Helms were not ready to turn Darla over to the public school system. At the Helms' request, Dr. Edge signed a statement that Darla was medically unfit and could not attend school. The school's solution was to send a home teacher to tutor Darla 3 hours a week. Rita Burton, teacher of the class for children with moderate handicaps in Winthrop, agreed to work with Darla after her school day ended.

Rita "worked wonders" with Darla in her 3 hours a week. She could get Darla's attention, make her sit and work, and, most important, got her to say eight words (up, down, sit, drink, eat, mom, baby, bye). According to Carol, Rita had a "tough-love" philosophy: She was strict and demanding in making Darla perform. According to Carol, she used the slang that parents use, threat-ening, "I'll beat your butt," "wring your neck," "smack you." But Carol knew that Rita would never hurt Darla; that she only used tough tactics to get Darla to respond. When Darla performed well, Rita would hug and kiss her and was generous with praise. Darla seemed pleased with her accomplishments and was eager to work with Rita. Carol loved Rita.

The following year, because of their trust in Rita and at Rita's urging, Carol and James allowed Darla to attend Rita's class for children with mod-erate disabilities, which happened to be in their neighborhood school. Darla was classified severely retarded, so Ingalls felt that the class for children with severe disabilities would have better suited her needs. But that class was 7 miles away in a neighboring town. Carol and James would not agree to busing her to the other school. The Helms' third child, Missy, was an infant, and Carol liked the convenience of driving both Darla and Jimmy, a second grader, to the neighborhood school. Carol also liked the fact that "Jimmy could look out for Darla."

On the grounds that they were sheltered and overprotected at home, Rita got her pupils out into the community to bowl, shop, and eat at restaurants. Because they felt Darla's hyperactivity and loud screaming would disturb others, James and Carol had rarely taken Darla shopping or to restaurants. They were delighted that Rita was so bold. Rita insisted that her students share the playground and attend gym, art, and music with their nonhandicapped peers. Rita was beloved by most of the parents of her pupils, but a few objected to her rough demeanor and language. Rita was a big, aggressive woman, who made demands not only of her pupils, but also of school officials. If administrators did not respond to her requests, she got parents involved. In spite of her success with her pupils, Rita was perceived as "unprofessional" by her supervisors, and her contract was not renewed. Carol was ready to fight for her reappointment, but Rita had recently married and decided to move out of state.

Carol reports that when Rita left, Darla's language left. Carol tried to imitate Rita's techniques with Darla, but Darla simply would not respond to Carol as she had to Rita. Rita was replaced by Janey Tellingho. On the surface, Janey was a mild-mannered person who dressed and looked like a "teacher." She never used slang or threats. But, unlike Rita, Janey used physical force with the children. Whereas Rita would tower over a student or firmly push a child into sitting position, no one ever observed Rita hit a child. Parents often accompanied Rita on class trips, so they knew how she operated. Janey was less open and less comfortable with parents. She kept her class out of sight. There were no more trips into the community. Janey went along with administrators' wishes and did not make "unreasonable" demands. School supervisors liked Janey. Carol hated her.

After being with Tellingho for almost a year, Darla had made no progress; in fact, she had regressed. Darla was becoming even more withdrawn from her peers. She spent much of her time pacing at the edges of the classroom. Whenever she had the opportunity, she darted away from the class. When someone moved into her space or made requests of her, Darla was likely to scratch them. Carol was disheartened at Darla's regression.

Carol had developed warm relationships with the two instructional aides in Darla's classroom during Rita's tenure, when she had been a frequent visitor to the class. The aides confided to Carol that Janey often got frustrated with the children's behaviors and hit, shook, or slammed children down into their seats. Although she had not done these things to Darla, she had strapped Darla into a chair for long periods of time. Carol tried to convince the aides to share their observations with administrators, but they were reluctant to get involved. So Carol reported their stories to the principal and Ken Ingalls. Neither took action. Ingalls's response was to try, again, to get the Helms to send Darla to the class for students with severe handicaps. Although they went to observe in that classroom, they refused to allow Darla to go there.

Determined and assertive when she felt that Darla was in danger or was not being properly taught, Carol was not going to sit back. She went to the school every day and sat and watched. When Tellingho complained, the principal accused Carol of obstructing the children's education and said she would have to leave the school. Carol refused. The principal called the police. The police supported Carol's right to observe in the classroom as long as she sat quietly. Eventually the school corporation built a one-way mirrored observation booth adjacent to the classroom, specifically for Carol. At about this time, 8-year-old Jimmy was so uncomfortable being in the same school as Darla that the Helms requested he be transferred to another school—a request that was promptly granted.

One day when Carol arrived to get Darla she noticed an "angry red hand mark" on Darla's face. When confronted, Janey admitted that she had slapped Darla. That was too much. Although Carol had heard stories of physical punishment involving other pupils, to her knowledge Darla had never been hit before. Carol went to the other parents to inform them of Janey's actions, and the next day all nine parents were in the classroom. Consequently Janey was fired. Carol was relieved, but at the same time she was bothered that she was "the most hated parent" in the school. Carol knew that she and her daughter were frequent topics of conversation throughout the school corporation because of Darla's bizarre behavior and Carol's assertive demands and confrontations with school officials. The school board knew about Carol because they were forced to construct the observation booth in the special education room and because of the demand for Tellingho's dismissal. Winthrop is a small town and the family had a reputation.

The Advice of Experts. The Helms pored through magazines and books for ideas for diagnoses and interventions, as well as for names of doctors or clinics that might help them with their problematic daughter. They experimented with "every conceivable" intervention at home. Darla had been on the Feingold diet, a dietary intervention usually prescribed for hyperactive, distractable children, which involved eliminating sugars and additives from a child's diet. They had tried hypnosis. Friends and relatives also continually gave advice and recommended specialists. Frustrated at every turn, Carol confided, "When you have a daughter like Darla, you try anything."

One of the problems in diagnosing autism is that the condition includes a broad range of characteristics and severity levels, but children can be diagnosed as autistic even when they have only a few of the symptoms. Therefore, in reading about autism, the Helms noted attributes that Darla did not have (e.g., fascination with motor sounds, echolalia), which gave them hope that she might not be autistic. Another characteristic of autism is that children tend to have an uneven profile of skills; that is, they have weaknesses in many areas and strengths in others. A vivid example is the exceptional mathematical calculation ability of the young man with autism in *Rainman*. Darla was mechanically advanced, although she was more likely to take things apart than put them together. The presence of certain strengths tends to make others believe that the individual is not really retarded, not really autistic. Moreover, the prognosis for children with autism is negative. Again, Carol was hopeful that Darla might be classified with a condition that was curable, or at least with one in which she would not regress. Throughout the time that Darla was in public school, the Helms continued their search for "someone to perform a miracle cure."

They heard about Dr. Martin Lynton, a diagnostic specialist, who directed a clinic on the east coast. They were barely surviving financially, but they were determined to do the best for Darla. Darla spent a week at Lynton's clinic undergoing a variety of tests. Influenced by the Helms' impression that Darla's condition had been getting progressively worse, Lynton suggested Darla might have a slow-growing brain tumor, so he ordered a CAT-scan. No tumor was found. All test results were negative. Carol confessed to "almost hoping for a tumor," because then there might be a surgical cure—a chance for improvement. According to Carol, Lynton's opinion was that Darla was "not retarded, not autistic, not schizophrenic"—that what Darla was "had not yet been invented." The trip had cost $10,000. They were livid.

One of their last trips was to a "freaky" clinic in a neighboring state. It turned out to be a more productive trip than their "more respectable" ventures. This clinic tested not only blood and urine, but skin, hair, and saliva. Clinic personnel concurred with the retarded and autistic diagnoses, and admitted they could not cure these conditions, but they discovered two problems they could treat: a dangerously high lead level and a difference of about 2 inches between one leg and the other. The high level of lead in Darla's bloodstream was confirmed at Winthrop Hospital, and medication to remove it from her system was effective. (Darla had pica, a condition in which nonedibles as well as edibles are eaten. Doctors cautioned them to watch what Darla put in her mouth—a very difficult task.) Her shorter leg was caused by the thigh bone being jammed up into the hip socket, a condition she had lived with for many years. A few trips to the chiropractor cured that problem. The unique gait that Carol thought was "cute" and a psychiatrist thought "indicated retardation" was corrected.

Special Care: Delaying the Decision. After Tellingho was dismissed, her aide Elise Yoder was promoted to teacher. Carol liked Elise and respected her teaching of the other eight children in the classroom, but she was not the headstrong and effective Rita. Elise had worked with Rita and she was the first to admit that she was not as successful with Darla as Rita had been. According to Elise, "Rita was one in a million." Elise admitted her ineffectiveness with Darla and urged Carol to send Darla to the class for severe/ profound disabilities. But Carol was stubborn. The problems with Tellingho, following the Mapleton clinic disaster, increased Carol's resolve to keep a careful watch over Darla. More than anyone, Carol was aware of Darla's frustrating and annoying behaviors. Carol and James loved Darla. She was their child. They would not abuse her, but they worried that an outsider would. They knew and respected Elise, and although they suspected Darla would not make much progress in her classroom, at least they trusted her not to physically mistreat their child.

During her 2 years in Yoder's class, Darla got stronger and faster. She could outpower and outrun her teachers. She had to be watched constantly on the playground and, even then, she often got away. Her teachers had to make sure anything potentially dangerous was kept out of her reach. She would eat anything and could poison herself or eat an object that would injure her mouth or stomach. She could be affectionate and cooperative, but she would suddenly reach out and scratch or pinch someone or pull hair. Elise's aides were afraid to work with Darla and left her to pace the room. Elise worked with Darla, but she had to spend a fair share of time with other students. Carol was grateful that, in spite of Darla's disruptive influence on the class, Elise did not ask to have Darla removed.

Close to the end of Elise's second year as teacher, Darla suddenly reached out and, with all her considerable might, gouged her fingernail into Elise's upper arm. The wound was deep and painful. Elise was sent to the emergency room of the local hospital for treatment. Carol felt terrible about Elise's injury and came to school to apologize to her. Elise knew that Darla had struck out of frustration and did not ask for her to be removed from the class, but the principal felt they had tolerated enough of Darla's behavior. He called Dr. Quail, the School Superintendent, and Mr. Ingalls, and it was decided that Darla would be expelled. Carol and Elise were both upset at the suspension and "cried together."

A few years earlier, Carol had heard about the Clay Center's program for children with autism from a friend whose son had been tested there. Although diagnosed as autistic, he had good verbal communication skills and was making reasonable academic progress in a class for children with mild handicaps in Winthrop. Ingalls had also been in contact with Clay Center personnel for advice about providing an appropriate education for Darla. Darla was tested at the Clay Center when she was 12, and Clay staff consulted with Yoder about Darla's program.

Carol and James were impressed with the Clay facilities and staff and considered sending Darla there. Since her expulsion, Darla had received 3 hours a week of tutoring at home, but she was typically uncooperative and unresponsive during these sessions. Because Darla was disruptive in public and the Helms did not want to burden others with her care, family life was restricted. Jimmy was not encouraged to be involved in activities. Darla was becoming more of a problem at home and continued to regress. Although it was tempting to think of family life without Darla, they were haunted by memories of mistreatment at the Mapleton clinic. Their lingering fears of abuse resulted in a lack of trust in residential care, and they postponed making a decision about the Clay Center.

Darla usually had been fairly cooperative and compliant at home, but now that she was there on a full-time basis, she appeared to be bored in the small space of the trailer. Because her behaviors at home deteriorated during the summer, in the fall the Helms finally decided to give the Clay Center a try. Ken Ingalls was to apply to the state to have them pay for Darla's education at the Clay Center, but the processing of the paperwork was delayed. Darla remained at home, with a homebound teacher, in the fall. Due to complaints by state department officials that this treatment was too restrictive, in the spring Ingalls hired a personal teacher and aide, and Darla returned to share the space of Yoder's classroom. The expense of this arrangement upset school board members, and their anger escalated when they learned that nobody considered this program effective anyway. Everyone pressured Ingalls to do the necessary paperwork and get the State Department's financial backing to send Darla to the Clay program. In discussing the year's delay, Carol said that she suspected that Ingalls was opposed to filing the application because he felt his staff ought to be able to deal with Darla. He once told Carol, "We can't do every little whim that you come up with." In the spring, when the paperwork still had not been submitted, Carol went over Ingalls's head to Superintendent Quail, as she had done on a number of other occasions. Quail said, "I know you'll push me and push me until I do something. The one who barks gets it done." He supported Carol in pressuring Ingalls to hurry up and finish the paperwork. At several points Carol expressed the opinion that school personnel saw her as a "pain" or a "problem," but she was not overly concerned—she wanted what was best for her daughter regardless of what anyone thought.

Perceptions of Darla's Condition

Carol claims that when she was "young" and first noticed Darla's problems, she had a number of theories about causes, most of which were self-blaming. Darla had seemed normal, even precocious, during her first year. By the age of 16 months Darla had some behavioral patterns that Carol considered atypical. Since there was a change in development, Carol assumed that she was doing something wrong to cause it. She worried that her two children's births were too close together—that Darla's regression was caused by an interruption in the bonding between mother and daughter. After the first few months of colic, Darla was a healthy baby, so Carol did not attribute the changes to illness. Darla fell out of her high chair once, but the doctor said her injury was minor. Besides, Darla's problems emerged gradually over a few months' time.

As the years went by, Carol was influenced by other people's opinions. Dr. Lovell, at the Mapleton center, had attributed Darla's behavior patterns to her "hate for her parents." Although Carol never totally believed this theory, it still added to her guilt. Carol felt that James's mother and father blamed her for Darla's condition. The fact that her brother was disabled added to Carol's perception that the condition might be "due to bad genes." As more specialists concurred with the diagnosis of autism and Carol learned more about the condition, her self-blame subsided. At the time of the interviews, Carol still harbored an element of doubt about whether autism was an accurate classification and said, "Something else is wrong somewhere." She now believes that the condition has genetic origins and, fortunately, is able to conclude that it is probably James's fault as well as her own. The guilt feelings have decreased over the years.

Carol has only recently come to believe that Darla's condition is permanent—that she will not become normal. According to Carol, even if a miracle cure for autism were found, Darla still would be severely influenced by her unusual childhood. Although pleased with the approach used at the Clay Center, Carol predicts that Darla will not be radically different as an adult. This acknowledgment has stimulated Carol to make plans for Darla's future. Since Darla is so healthy and well-supervised, Carol assumes that she will outlive her parents. She hopes that Darla will improve enough to be in a group home, but worries that she will end up in a state institution. Carol's worst fear is that Darla will be "put in an insane asylum, where she will be abused and neglected."

Darla's Impact on Family Relationships

Carol states in a pained but somewhat resigned tone that friends are "few and far between," commenting: "People think that what Darla has is catching. Darla scares people. They do not want their children around her. People come over once and you never hear from them again. But we're used to it. It doesn't bother us anymore." Carol does resent her other children's "suffering because of people's prejudices."

Carol calls Jimmy a "loner," then clarifies that he has not belonged to sports or social groups because of the family's preoccupation with Darla's needs. When he was younger, Jimmy complained that the family did not go out to movies and restaurants like other families. He wanted his parents to come to school events, but the Helms felt that Darla could not accompany them, and they had no one to care for her. Carol recalled that sometimes Jimmy would beg: "Why can't you come?" But, for the most part, he understood that it was hard for his parents to cope with his sister. On the other hand, Carol was convinced that Jimmy got plenty of attention when he needed it—that they "made up for Darla" by buying him whatever he wanted: "Jimmy just makes a Christmas list and he gets everything on it."

Jimmy always made good grades and is known as a model citizen—well-behaved, polite, and responsible—in school. In his first year of high school, he made As and Bs in every subject except social studies, which he did not like. Carol thinks that Jimmy would like to go to college. Carol says he is well-liked by his classmates and teachers. Jimmy is also a skilled mechanic and "has been able to fix his own motorcycle since he was seven." In the summer and on weekends he works in his dad's machine shop and "makes repairs that stump the adult employees."

Carol has conflicted feelings about Darla's impact on the family. Sometimes she asserts that Darla has not affected Jimmy and Missy; then she turns around and poignantly details their pain and suffering. She very infrequently expresses resentment about Darla. In contrast, she seems almost angry at her other two offspring—particularly Jimmy—because they are normal and Darla is not. From an early age Jimmy took responsibility for his sister. He was competent in all the ways that she was not, and his parents continually reminded him of his duty to family and sister. When they were young he pushed Darla on the swing and played a version of swing the statue with her, which consisted mainly of grabbing her arm and pulling her around the yard. He would wrestle with her. Darla particularly liked to "arm wrestle" with her brother, a game that consisted of locking hands and fingertips and shoving each other around. Both children liked to wrestle. At times Darla would go up to Jimmy as if to say, "I want to play." When she had a toy that she was unable to make work, she would go to Jimmy and get him to help her.

In contrast to Carol's perception, Elise Yoder believes that Jimmy had to make a number of sacrifices because of Darla. He was transferred to another school when he was in third grade because being in the same school with his sister embarrassed him. Elise thinks that Darla should have been transferred to the school that all the professionals—herself included—thought would have been more appropriate for her. Elise also feels that Jimmy had been made to take responsibility for Darla at such a young age that it might have been difficult for him physically and emotionally. She did not see any indications that he resented Darla, but she conjectures that most kids in his situation would feel some anger and resentment, if not toward his sister, then toward his parents. Elise says that she tried to get up her nerve to talk to Carol about Jimmy's needs. She was bothered that Jimmy did not have more of a life of his own; that he was not allowed to be more childish. Darla was 11 months older than Jimmy, and remained bigger until he grew taller than she when they were about 13 and 14.

Although Carol usually denies that Jimmy suffered from the family situation, she also contradicts herself, confessing that she sometimes feels guilty about the impact she and James allowed Darla to have on the family. Once she launched into this account:

> Jimmy got left out in the cold. Darla's condition made him grow up quickly. If I had to go to the bathroom, I would say, "Jimmy, you watch Darla." Darla got attention while he stood by. Darla could be rough. He was not allowed to hurt her back because she was special. It was hell to live here. It changed his life. We were trapped. There was no way out. She would go haywire in public, so we could not go anywhere. Jimmy talks, talks, talks at home—is a holy terror—but they say he's quiet at school. He hasn't had to deal with the public and learn how to be comfortable and outgoing with others. But now that Darla is at the Clay Center he's learning quickly. We went to our first walk-in movie together. We have gone out to eat. We went to the roller skating rink with Jimmy and saw him skate for the first time. Jimmy handled responsibility well—he took it like a man.

In Carol's opinion, Missy is more outgoing and social in school, but her grades are not as good as Jimmy's were at her age. She has trouble with spelling, for example, and Carol has to help her learn her words; Jimmy did his homework independently. Carol feels that, like Jimmy, Missy is fond of Darla. Missy especially likes to play school with Darla: Missy takes the teacher role and bosses Darla around. Carol is amused that Darla tends to do what Missy commands. When Carol tells Missy to "leave Darla alone," Missy will say, "But Mom, Darla likes it." And Darla does seem to like the interaction with Missy. When Missy gets particularly loud and bossy, Darla laughs.

When Darla went to the Clay Center, Missy received more attention at home from her parents. When Darla was home, however, her needs came first. If Missy and Carol were doing something together, Darla often did something that required Carol's attention. Many stories were left half-read. Jimmy is less assertive than Missy. Before Darla's pregnancy, when his mother or father left him to take care of Darla, he never complained. Missy is more open about her emotions, voicing resentment if she does not get what she considers to be her fair share. If Missy does not like something, she tells people about it.

Carol feels that both Jimmy and Missy are used to Darla; living with her has been the only life they know. When Missy went to kindergarten, Carol learned that she often asked other children about their big sisters. She assumed everyone had a big sister at home who could not talk and who acted like Darla. She was surprised to learn that she was unique. When Darla went to the Clay Center, Missy was upset and missed her. Jimmy had reacted similarly when Darla went to the Mapleton center when he was five. Both expressed concern that Darla had been sent away because she had been bad. Carol conjectured that they were frightened that they might be sent away too. All three children were fond of each other, and, although Darla might pinch or scratch adults, she was less likely to be aggressive toward her siblings or other children.

Carol's mother and father always accepted Darla. Carol's father liked horses, and when Darla was young he carefully led her around the yard on a pony. He had different expectations for Jimmy. He was more strict and pressed him to achieve and take chances on the pony. He helped Darla, but made Jimmy do things on his own.

Carol's mother, Dot, is a constant source of help and support for the family. (Carol called her mother a "doll." She said her mother would accept any kid—that she likes kids—but she especially likes her grandkids.) She loves all three children, but Darla is her "real baby." Darla needs more attention than the others, she demands it, and in Grandma's opinion she deserves it, so she gets it. Even now, when Darla is so much bigger than her grandmother, Dot will rock Darla in a rocker and let Darla play "horsey" on her knee. Darla is the special child who gets special love. At least once a month, Dot comes and stays with the family or they visit her. When James is unable to accompany Carol to take Darla somewhere, Dot "drops everything" to come and help.

James's parents live in Winthrop about 2 minutes away from the Helms, but, according to Carol, they act like Darla and the rest of the family do not exist. They are polite and check on Darla's well-being about once a month, but generally avoid the family. Carol speculates that this is because of Darla. They have never offered help with child care. When Darla's problems first became apparent, they tended to blame her behavior on Carol's child-rearing abilities. They couldn't blame their son's genes, so they blamed Carol. Carol reminisced that "when you're 17 and insecure, you believe that you're at fault. They really hurt me and I haven't gotten over it." Carol calls them "narrow-minded" and "cruel."

Darla's Influence on Her Parents' Marriage

Carol calls her husband and herself "family people." The family is their responsibility and it comes first. Carol judges James to be even more family-oriented than she is. Having Darla has brought them closer together. During the years when they were seeking treatment, they both were involved; they had to stick together to battle for Darla. In Carol's opinion nobody willingly gave Darla help—she and James had to fight for everything they got for Darla. Carol's anger is directed at people who did not do well by Darla. Carol and James usually agree about what is best for Darla. Although James's parents blame Carol for Darla's condition, James does not. He has always been sensitive to Carol's feelings and defended her against his parents.

Carol and James were teenagers when they became parents of two children. They took on responsibility early. There was neither time nor money for them to have "much fun" together. They always "wondered what it would be like to go out." That part of raising Darla made it rough. They took turns going out. However, they never went out for fun, only for shopping or to school functions. Within the last year before Darla went to the Clay Center, they began to leave Jimmy at home to care for his two sisters. They felt that he was responsible and mature enough to be in charge. James and Carol definitely enjoyed their outings and time alone together.

In spite of what Carol described as "missed good times" because of Darla, Carol said she really did not feel sorry for herself. She would change Darla if she could—make her normal—but she would not make her abnormal daughter disappear. There were good times and there was lots of family love.

Darla's Influence on Religious Beliefs

Carol's anger at Darla's condition has influenced her religious beliefs. She says friends and relatives have accused both her and James of being atheists because they no longer believe in God. James's family are Seventh Day Adventists and Carol was raised a Baptist, but their faith has gradually eroded. Carol said that she had never been very religious, but went to church with her family and believed in God. Since the early years of their marriage they have asked questions that could not be answered, and over the years their religious feelings crumbled. She believes there is no God or, if there is, he is bad and wrong. Carol mentions that, at various times, she has received pamphlets from different churches claiming that she has been chosen by God to be the parent of a special child because she is a special person. Her response to that message is "bullshit!"

Carol is not entirely sure that they would have been "good Christians" even if they had not had Darla. She always had a certain disdain for churchgoers who seemed more interested in appearance and social status than religion. Coming from a poor family, Carol always felt a little out of place in church and thought that others looked down on her. Carol has more respect for the Seventh Day Adventists, because she believes they live their religion more sincerely. She said that most of the people in that church are poor and that they wear their farm clothes to church and do not notice what other people wear. If she were to rejoin a congregation she would be tempted to join the Seventh Day Adventists.

JAMES'S STORY

James was born 20 miles away from Winthrop, in a small town just across the state border. His family moved frequently during his childhood, but they rarely went more than 25 miles from his place of birth. Around the time James was married, his family moved to Winthrop, and James and Carol followed them there. During both his adolescence and adult life James worked off and on for his father. About 2 years prior to Darla's going to the Clay Center, James bought a machine shop from his father. Apparently the senior Mr. Helm was having serious financial problems. James offered to restructure the shop and eventually ended up as the owner and person in charge. A good deal of family friction resulted from this takeover, which James attributed to miscommunication and jealousy, but he feels that the problems are gradually being resolved.

James was the eldest of four, with two brothers and a sister. Of his childhood James recalled that he was "pushed hard" and had a lot "laid on" him, that he "had no childhood" and was "forced to grow up too soon." As the oldest child he was "given too much responsibility too early," which James said was "not right" and "not fair." Besides being given responsibility for the care of his younger brothers and sister when he was in his early teens, James's mechanical abilities were acknowledged and he was expected to do the work of a man. James's father was not always successful with his various enterprises, so James worried about his family staying financially afloat. Although he felt that he was respected by his parents and siblings, James often suspected that they resented him or had unrealistic expectations about what he should do for them, instead of rewarding him for his efforts on the family's behalf.

With the exception of a certain scorn for his father's lack of business skill, James spoke fondly of his dad. He described his father as "basically a good man" whose main problem was being heavily influenced by his mother. James was not inclined to be generous in talking about his mother. He called her a "manic depressive," a "back biter," and a "griper," who has something bad to say about everybody and everything. According to James, his mother was always difficult to get along with. James felt lonely and had no friends as a child, not only because he had work responsibilities, but also because his mother alienated potential friends. James recalls that kids would come over once, meet his mother, and would then stay away. Additionally, James accuses his mother of being a "snob" who considers herself to be "too good" for everybody. After making these remarks, James adds: "Mom is basically a good woman who has a hard time with everybody. She can't make or keep friends."

In spite of his bitterness about having no friends and being a "loner" during his childhood, James has a great sense of family loyalty and maintains a fairly close relationship with the parents about whom he and his wife feel so ambivalent. James realizes that Carol frequently has been hurt by her mother-in-law's jabs and barbs and he faithfully takes Carol's side in disputes.

Looking back, James recognizes that his mother actively disliked Carol during the first years of their marriage. In the first place Mrs. Helm did not want James to marry Carol. Then, when Darla's problems began to surface, she blamed them on Carol. This was particularly painful for Carol, who in the first few years had a tendency to blame herself for Darla's condition. Mrs. Helm reinforced Carol's feelings of inadequacy as a mother. Gradually, as Carol became convinced that Darla was more than just spoiled, and as she observed her own successful mothering with Jimmy, she gained confidence in her parenting ability and realized that her mother-in-law's negative judgments were totally unjustified. Much of Mrs. Helm's criticism was so subtle that James did not notice, but Carol always did. Eventually, Carol started to fight back, and James encouraged her to speak up and defend herself against his mother's tongue.

James laughed delightedly as he recalled confrontations between Carol and his mother and praised Carol for "putting Mom in her place." A couple of years earlier, Carol had become so angry at Mrs. Helm that she had driven over to her in-laws' home with the intention to "whoop their butts." She "bawled them out" for about 2 hours, even though they attempted to "throw Carol out." Carol summarized all the injustices that had occurred through the years and she "laid down the law" for their future relationships. She would not leave until she had finished saying all that she wanted to say, and, according to James, who was not present at this showdown, she "really nailed them" and they "got what they deserved." (One has the hunch that James exults vicariously in Carol's recently gained ability to stand up to his parents, while he remains the dutiful son.) James relished relating that the confrontation "almost caused his mother to have a heart attack. She was so shocked."

James's parents kept their distance for a long while after Carol's verbal attack, but since then interactions have been fairly polite and respectful. Strangely enough, James felt that it was Darla's pregnancy that started to bring the extended family back together after the rift, even though it had a divisive impact on his immediate family. Although the senior Helms did not help during Darla's pregnancy, they "kept their mouths shut" when they visited and did not interfere with James and Carol's decisions. For the first time they seemed to respect the younger Helms' right to make their own plans. However, in contrast to James's feeling that previous family conflicts had subsided, he felt that Carol continued to feel implied criticism in her mother-in-law's presence—that past resentments still smoldered.

Except for one brother, James's siblings live in Winthrop, and even that brother divides his time between Winthrop and a western state. James describes both brothers as "wild" and "rough" and his sister as only more subtly so. He categorizes his brothers as "Harley-types" (i.e., they ride motorcycles and act tough). James's brother Dale lives with his girlfriend about a mile away from the Helms in the trailer park where James and Carol and their children used to live. Dale works for James, who alludes to difficulties with him in the boss/employee realm. James even suggests that he might have to "fire" his brother, although he does not specify why. He mentions a problem with drugs and alcohol among his employees in general, and one suspects that this may be Dale's problem. According to James, Dale intentionally gained about 40 pounds to have a "beer belly" and "look more macho and tough." Dale wears heavy boots and leather jackets and vests, and has "garbage (chains and metal objects) hanging all over him." James describes Dale's boozing and carousing and says he "lives with a woman, but never lets her know where he is or when he's coming home." Carol is friendly with Dale's girlfriend, who was willing to babysit for Darla occasionally. James laughs as he describes his brother, but one sees evidence of concern on the part of the responsible older brother. He shakes his head and says that Dale is "crazy" and has "severe problems," but he does not disclose exactly what "the kid's" problems are.

Although James does not have much to say about his sister, Denise, he refers to her as "a woman who knows how to have a good time." Denise has been dating a fellow who owns a local bar and pool hall, and James admits that "Denise spends a lot of time there." James recalls that when Darla was about 13 years old, Denise convinced James and Carol that they needed to get out more, saying, "You kids need to learn to have fun." Carol and James started to go out with Denise and her boyfriend fairly regularly. They would drink and often stayed out until 3 or 4 in the morning. Before that, because of child-care problems, they only went out for dinner on their anniversary and Carol's birthday and were never gone for more than an hour or two. James's parents rarely volunteered to babysit for the children, although James felt that his father was "good as gold" with them. The children, especially Darla, made his mother too nervous and she was a "wreck" even when they went out for only short periods of time. They did not feel they could impose on the local teenagers because Darla was such a handful; therefore they mainly watched television together at home. Occasionally they took the family to a drive-in movie or fast-food restaurant, but even this was difficult because Darla would become upset and unmanageable.

James is genuinely fond of Dot, Carol's mother, calling her a "darn good girl" who helped tremendously through the years. Her only fault is that "she's the nervous type, panic-minded, who often goes off the deep end or flies off the handle." However, James added, "she is very strong at the same time." James felt that she always respected their decisions and supported them 100 percent when she could.

James said that when he first met Will, his father-in-law, he judged him to be "about as low as they come," claiming "he would do anything to anybody for a buck." He was well-known to police in their corner of the state and plenty of times would get into trouble for resisting arrest. He got into fist fights on the slightest provocation. According to James, Dot suffered because of him.

> Will played around. When he heard of a rich widow he would start a relationship and con her out of a truck or some tools. Dot just tolerated all of his behaviors but they hurt her and Carol too. When Will turned 40 he started to have heart problems and he calmed down. During the last few years, Will became the sweetest man, a real family man who was loving to his wife, daughter, and grandchildren.

Will made it clear that he resented James marrying his daughter, but when his health declined he made an effort at reconciliation. They got along fine after that. James felt that he had earned his father-in-law's respect by staying with Carol after Darla became such a problem. In fact, just before he died, Will specifically thanked James for "being so good to Carol and Darla." James felt that Will, like Dot, would have done anything for Darla.

James was 34 when Darla came to the Clay Center. Clay staff described him as good looking and surprisingly young, dressed in tight-fitting jeans, a leather jacket, and boots, and with a head of dark brown hair. They remarked that his intimate manner of speaking to women, regardless of their age or appearance, was striking but did not bother them. The female staff generally found him to be a congenial, likable person and not necessarily sexist in approach. The interviewer commented that she felt that he clearly enjoyed female company and was willing to talk more openly about his past and his feelings than one might expect from men. He also has a warm and gentle sense of humor and tends to tease about touchy subjects, but his comments are never sarcastic or belligerently directed toward people that he perceives as attempting to be helpful. Although appearing calm and easy-going, he is intense and conveys determination and independence. Only the chain smoking and the tick and muscle spasms that occasionally distort his face suggest the strain of a difficult life.

Feelings About His Marriage

When asked about his marriage, James pauses for quite a while and then says:

> It's been a good marriage—one of the best—but it's had its ups and
> downs. Right now the last thing I would tell anyone is to get married
> and have kids. It's a mistake for people under 23 or 24 to have chil-
> dren. Oh, they can do a good job, it's not that, but between 18 and 23
> there are other things to experience. If you don't experience them
> then, you'll hurt the rest of your life. You'll never get another chance.
> But Carol and me chose to get married. We did not have to. I was still
> in high school when we married. At first we were going to postpone
> having kids, but the doctor told Carol that she would have a hard time
> getting pregnant. Carol was upset. I told her that she was going to
> have children no matter what. It became a challenge to prove the
> doctor wrong. So, Darla was a "very planned" baby, but we really had
> originally intended to wait.

About Carol, James brags:

> God never made a better woman; very smart, good, good-natured.
> She always works hard. With Carol the kids come first—they come
> before me. She likes all kids but she is protective about her kids—you
> don't mess with them, don't hurt them or you'll be in trouble. She
> likes being with the kids. She plays with them and helps with their
> homework. Even when she does not feel well she will get up and do
> things for the family. She is a fine mother. That is why she never gave
> up with Darla.

After receiving the news of Darla's pregnancy, the Helms' social life
stopped. However, within a few months, James succumbed to the invitation
of a long-term customer/friend, who for some time had been coaxing him to
"go get a beer." James did not call Carol, thinking that he would be out only
for about half an hour, but he proceeded to get drunk and did not get home
until 3 or 4 in the morning. During the next few months, he repeated this
behavior on a weekly basis. James admits that he feels guilty about his binges,
but he gets tense at work and is not eager to go home where he knows there
will be more friction. James says that he needs something besides work and
television and he finds that playing pool and having a few beers with his
brother in a bar is relaxing. He often goes with the intention of staying for
half an hour and having one beer; then he finds that it turns into a "4–5 hour

deal." James hints that Dale likes company, but is not a very good influence on him.

Another night James stayed at a local club drinking for a long time and a woman there flirted with him. He took her to another bar. Someone who was at the local club called Carol to tell her that she "better go after her husband," who was both drunk and with another woman. Carol went to the bar and "embarrassed" him by "making a scene." James left the bar in his truck and drove drunkenly away at top speed. He smashed the truck and severed a telephone pole about 10 feet above the ground. Amazingly, he was uninjured and crawled out of a window in the truck and let Carol, who had been following in her car, drive him home. The truck is now parked in the machine shop and James works on repairing it when he has time. James believes that his behavior was the result of depression.

Feelings About Darla

James said the category autistic is the closest you could get in terms of labeling Darla, although he believes there are several reasons why the classification is not a "true fit." James also refers to Darla as "severely retarded." He said that some doctors have classified her as schizophrenic, but he tends not to agree with that label for Darla, mainly because he does not agree with the treatment that Darla received from the professionals who diagnosed her as schizophrenic.

James contends that being "just a kid" himself when Darla was born prevented him from being more aware earlier that she had serious problems. Looking back, after raising two normal children, he feels that Darla was always different and difficult. As an infant she was discontented. When Darla was somewhat over a year old, shortly after Jimmy was born, James and Carol were worried enough about Darla's development that, although they continued to use Wilder for routine pediatric care, they started calling and visiting other doctors. Each time, when they found that their concerns were not taken seriously or when no solutions were offered for her problems, they would try someone else. James remembers that when Darla was about a year old, her high chair tipped over, knocking her unconscious. James said they felt guilty about the accident, especially when Darla began having grand mal seizures, but doctors assured them that they found no evidence of brain injury and did not think her problems were the result of a fall. Carol and James realized the extent of Darla's delayed development when at about one year Jimmy began to surpass his 2-year-old sister in many developmental areas.

James's descriptions of their search for services for Darla were similar to Carol's: "We pretty much exhausted the resources. We tried everything." James had a cynical view of individuals in the medical profession and at the administrative level of service provision for the developmentally disabled population. Although he praised social workers and teachers—in fact, all direct contact workers—he was of the opinion that administrators are "out to make a buck" and they are "using handicapped people to collect." James contends that he worked with politicians for a while and thought they were a "pack of rats." According to James, the first couple of years he dealt with Hudson County administrators and the school board trying to get services for Darla, he did not understand their reasoning. Once he realized they were "political," he felt he better understood their motives and how he needed to interact with them "to get anything out of them." James reads the financial reports in the local paper and can reel off figures from memory. In his opinion the school spends "ungodly amounts of money" and by "cheating here and there," administrators and the board "line their pockets." James notes that the special education budget practically doubled every year for 4 years, even though services were not expanded. James believes he and Carol had to fight for every service because the administration reasoned that the less they spent on students the more they could personally collect. As he sardonically observed, "Tell people that there is a retarded child and they start collecting."

In this regard, James particularly resents Ken Ingalls, who he feels did not file the papers with the state for Darla to start at the Clay Center because he wanted to keep her in his "head count" so he could "collect on her." James was more positive about Superintendent Quail, who he felt "at least realized that we were right about what we wanted for Darla." He also felt that Quail could not be "too open" because he was "protecting Ingalls." James reported that there no longer were special education classes in Winthrop and that they "bused all the handicapped children to a special school in a town at the other end of the three-county special education cooperative" about 40 miles away. He saw this as the administration's move to "save money," although he was sure that the "state would not save a dime." James suggests that the superintendent agreed to this arrangement to avoid embarrassing publicity about the low quality of local special education services, the consequence of Ingalls's poor administration over the years.

James was 18 when Darla was born, and at 19 he was the father of two children. He was trying to support his family and trying to understand and do something about his firstborn's problem. Every medical opinion they received and program they entered cost money. They pulled up roots and traveled far afield to find the best authorities. Yet, in spite of their expenditure of time, money, energy, and emotion, they found no remedies for Darla's condition. Perhaps the years of frustration resulted in what James admits is "paranoia" and a tendency to be "prone to suspicion." He emphasized several times that the "money deal" really bothers him. He himself has spent a great deal of money and has not seen a significant improvement in Darla. James said:

> You can have great teachers but under the thumbs of administrators they don't get what they need. Darla has not gotten the benefit of the money that was supposed to help her. You never get more than one-third of the money you are entitled to; they pocket the rest. . . . The biggest frustration in having an autistic daughter is having to deal with corrupt characters. That is the cause of 30–40% of the headaches in my life.

James maintains that partly because of her effectiveness, the spokesperson role for the family was turned over to Carol fairly early in their marriage. He describes Carol as "the best arguer I've ever seen." According to James, "Carol raises hell; she is stubborn and stands her ground. If she has full understanding of the situation, you would not want to oppose her." James feels that at first Carol was "gullible"; administrators "sounded good" and she did "not want to believe that her opposition was crooked." Once she understood with whom she was dealing, she learned to stand her ground and became really good at interacting with administrators. He and Carol often talked about "tactics" at home and then Carol would go off to school and "do something about the situation" the next day.

James believes that Darla definitely influenced Carol's personality and outlook on life, as well as his own. He believes that dealing with others on Darla's account has made them strong, realistic, and better able to understand themselves and others. James believes he is now less likely to be bashful and afraid of others. This change in his personality, he feels, also affects his relationships with friends, relatives, and business associates. James considers himself to be a shrewd observer of others. He has grown assertive in relationships, even with his own parents, who used to "boss him around." James laughs as he describes himself as "strong-headed" and confesses that the extent of this characteristic is "beyond my own good at times."

Outsiders disagree about who is the more dominant of the two and about who makes decisions in the family. When asked about this contradiction, James laughs and replies, "You know, there has recently been a lot of discussion about this in my family. I don't think that you can split 'being the boss' 50/50. If you do that, you argue all the time and never are able to make a decision. I told Carol that I wanted a 60/40 split and that I get the 60." One senses that he really feels that Carol had the 60 and he the 40. James claims that he and Carol always agree on what is best for Darla. They both worry about her welfare and prefer to keep her with them at home. They are united in what they perceive as a war against others on Darla's behalf. Like Carol, James concludes that Darla made their marriage stronger and brought them closer together.

James contends that children with autism are the most difficult kind of handicapped children to raise, with the exception, he speculates, of children with major medical difficulties. James mentions that they know a boy with spina bifida; James pities his mother for the mothering role she must assume with him. James feels that because autistic children "look so normal," it is hard to believe that their condition cannot be reversed and their difficulties overcome. James states that it took them 13 years to decide that Darla was "permanently" handicapped. He feels that they now accept "the fact" that her condition is not curable and that their daughter will be similar to the way she is now all her life. Coming reluctantly to this conclusion, he feels that they are now ready to turn the care of their daughter over to other people. They had experienced major problems with Darla at home during her thirteenth year, and with her suspension from school, they did not even have partial-day respite from their daughter. The strain of the year and their own lack of success with Darla convinced them that she should leave home to go to the Clay Center.

James said that they had been talking about building a home for many years. In the past, James said he always visualized the house as having one large room, about one-third the size of the whole house, built specifically for Darla. Lately, he admits, when he thinks about houses he does not imagine Darla's special room. When he became aware of his unconscious exclusion of his daughter, he was mostly relieved that she was no longer foremost in his thoughts and plans.

James says that they love Darla and wanted her home when she was younger. They were incensed when others recommended that she be institutionalized. They felt that she was their responsibility and they fought for the best for her. But she was a constant worry and had to be watched every moment of the day. In retrospect, James concludes that they "carried the whole thing too far." James says that he and Carol sometimes got so involved in "the fight" that they could not make good decisions, admitting, "I fought like hell all the time, why? Hell, I probably should have fought the other direction most of the time. It was one little battle after another." James admits some regrets about not having Darla in a program away from home.

James credits the Clay Center with enabling him to make the transition to allow his daughter more independence and to take a more distant, objective stance regarding her. He feels that the Clay staff really care about Darla and have her best interests in mind. Therefore, he and Carol can relax, forget about Darla to some extent, and think about the rest of the family for a change: "Clay staff are the only people that we have ever really trusted Darla with; we love and trust all those people at the Clay Center." He said that they were at peace when Darla was gone, knowing that she was receiving humane and beneficial care, although he did not expect Clay to "perform miracles" with Darla. When asked if he felt that he had made any mistakes in the past with Darla or if there was anything he would do differently if he had the chance to do things over again, James said that he would have sent her to the Clay Center 5 years earlier, when she was first found to be eligible for the residential program. James felt that Darla would have made more progress and he added, "If she had gone there sooner, the rest of us would not be going through the suffering that we are now."

Darla was already about 5 months pregnant when Clay staff called James to inform him of her pregnancy. James said that he was stunned by the news, that it came as a complete surprise. James immediately assumed that his daughter would have an abortion. He could not conceive of her going through the birth of a baby—that an abortion would be easier for Darla than giving birth to a full-term baby. However, James said that when he and Carol talked to doctors, they were told that the pregnancy was in too advanced a stage for an abortion to be safely performed.

CHAPTER 3

Professionals' Perceptions of Darla

Our original intentions were to document the events surrounding Darla's pregnancy and the birth of her son. However, during the interviews with James and Carol Helm, they both described years of sometimes congenial, but mainly contentious, relations with school and medical personnel. The Helms were the first to suggest that we interview others who interacted with the family. They seemed to want verification of their views of Darla and of what happened with her through the years.

BEFORE THE PREGNANCY

The interviews with professionals commenced soon after Darla's pregnancy was discovered and continued through the first year following her son's birth. All individuals interviewed were aware of Darla's pregnancy, but the paternity of her baby was not established until after they were completed.

Winthrop School Personnel

Three Winthrop school personnel were interviewed about Darla: Hudson County School Superintendent Dr. Fred Quail, Special Education Director Ken Ingalls, and Elise Yoder, who had been an aide in Darla's special education class when Darla was 10 and 11 and then her classroom teacher the 2 subsequent years. Two state education department officials were also interviewed about their roles in relation to Darla and her family. Linda Paskin worked for Protection and Advocacy in the State Education Department. Susan Andrews was a State Consultant for Emotional Handicaps and had administrative responsibility for placement in programs such as the Clay Center.

Dr. Quail, born and raised in Winthrop, had taught in the system and had lesser administrative roles before becoming superintendent, a position he had assumed 10 years prior to his interview. He estimated that he had known the Helm family for about 6 years. He had a vivid memory of the first day he met Darla. Carol and James Helm had come to his office to talk to him about appropriate services for Darla and had brought Darla along. Darla, who was about 9 years old at the time, sat passively in his office while the three adults talked, but at one point she quietly got up and went over to straighten a picture on his wall. That act made a lasting impression on Dr. Quail.

Over the next few years, Dr. Quail met or talked on the phone with Carol Helm several times a year. She had, he felt, unusually high expectations for her daughter, although he commented that this is "typical of parents." He thought Carol's goals for Darla were "unusually unreasonable"—she assumed that by the time Darla was 16 or 17 years old she would be normal, and the schools were to accomplish this feat. Quail felt the Helms' prospects for Darla had "neutralized" over time, but complained that they continued to have high expectations of all professionals and were assertive in initiating contacts with the school and making demands. Quail said they continually complained that their daughter was not getting a proper education. He was annoyed that the school corporation had been forced to build the one-way glass observation booth in Darla's classroom specifically for Carol. Quail also described the Helms as "overprotective" and was amazed that they would not let Darla ride a school bus to the class for children with severe disabilities in a school "just 7 miles down the road."

In spite of having to deal frequently with what he felt were unrealistic and unreasonable requests, Dr. Quail was genuinely fond of Mrs. Helm, whom he described as basically "pleasant to deal with." He felt that often she just wanted to "unload her feelings" on someone. He felt sorry for Carol, had compassion for what she was going through, and admired her assertiveness in getting the best for her daughter. He stated that he tried to accommodate the Helms, as he did all parents, whenever he could.

Quail had observed Darla on a number of occasions as he visited the schools in his district. He commented that her behavior in school varied from one time to the next. Sometimes she sat passively and at other times she would be running, pacing, or screaming. He noted that she "liked to run" and teachers worried that she would get away from them. He felt that basically "she wanted to do what she wanted to do when she wanted to do it," and if she didn't get her way she bit and became unmanageable. He "rated Darla" as "presenting more problems" to Winthrop schools than any other student. There was, he said, "no one else like her." The teachers complained about Darla and told stories about things she had done, but they never asked to have her removed from their classes. He felt this was because he had a dedicated special education staff.

Quail had not received any specialized training in dealing with people with disabilities during his professional schooling, but did not necessarily feel incompetent in this area. He trusted his special education staff to help him make decisions and had particular respect for Ken Ingalls, who had been Special Education Director for the Tri-County Special Education Cooperative for 13 years.

Ken Ingalls first interacted with James and Carol Helm when Darla was 6 years old and was at the Mapleton clinic. Carol Helm had called Ingalls to check on local programs in the hope that Darla could come home to live. Ken categorized Carol as "suffering from separation anxiety." He recalled that she had criticized the Mapleton clinic on several grounds, but seemed to be most concerned about the high levels of medication that Darla was receiving. Darla stayed at Mapleton until late spring, then lived at home for the remainder of the school year. The next fall Ingalls threatened the Helms with child neglect if they did not enroll her in school. Eventually, after they produced a medical certificate, he allowed Darla to stay at home and provided a homebound teacher, Rita Burton.

Ken Ingalls guessed that he had talked to the Helms, particularly Carol, at least 10 to 20 times a year during the 9 years between his initial contact with them and the time he was interviewed for this study. Ingalls seconded Quail's appraisal of the Helms as "very protective" of Darla. He, too, had been frustrated and annoyed because they would not give permission for her to attend a class for severely handicapped youngsters in a neighboring town, even though they agreed that it would be a more suitable program for Darla. Ingalls felt that part of their reluctance stemmed from their negative experiences at Mapleton. The Helms were simply unwilling to let Darla be very far away from them. Yet, as she grew older, Darla was becoming more difficult to manage, and the teachers of the various classrooms where she was placed constantly reminded Ingalls that their curriculum was not appropriate for her needs. The teachers pointed out that they had to use their classroom aides solely to work with Darla, when they felt the aides' services should be more evenly distributed among the children.

By the time she was 13, Darla had become a major behavior management problem, and Ingalls strongly recommended some form of residential program. The Helms visited the Clay Center and had Darla evaluated there. Even at that time they expressed a concern that if Darla lived there they would not want her left alone with male college students who were employed in the residential program. In spite of their visit to the Clay Center, they chose to keep Darla at home that year. When things continued to go downhill, and Darla was suspended from school, Carol first decided to work with Darla herself until things "settled down." Shortly thereafter, Carol requested that

Ingalls do the necessary paperwork for the Clay Center, stating that they wanted her there "as soon as possible."

In order for Darla to attend the Clay Center, Ingalls had to file a special regulation request with the State Department of Education asking for a state interagency agreement to allow the provision of state funds for residential treatment for a student whose needs could not be met by the local school corporation. For some unknown reason, Ingalls did not file the regulation request when he said he would. The paperwork sat in his desk drawer for more than 7 months. A year later Carol continued to resent this procrastination, and added that the "pregnancy probably wouldn't have happened" if Ingalls had been more "on the ball." Ingalls knew that the Helms were annoyed at him, but he could not explain why he did not file the application. Perhaps it was because he had little hope that the Helms would consent to sending their daughter away when the time actually came. Quail shrugged his shoulders about this incident and simply commented: "He just didn't do it. I had to get after him to get it done. I guess he doesn't like paperwork."

Later that year, Darla was found eligible for state funding and the Helms gave their consent. Darla began at the Clay Center in the fall, a couple of months after her fifteenth birthday. Ingalls claimed that he would have filed a child neglect complaint, based on the parents not allowing Darla to have an appropriate education, if the Helms had not agreed to send her to the Clay Center.

Ingalls was sure that he had interacted with the Helms more than with any other set of parents during his administrative career. It was the only case in which he had filed a regulation request. He felt the Helms were often "mad at him" for one thing or another, but especially when he did not file the application fast enough after they finally decided that "they wanted her out of the house." Ingalls was not sure why they suddenly changed their minds, but speculated it was because Darla was so difficult to deal with at home and they finally just got "worn out." Although Ingalls frequently was upset with the Helms, he was particularly fond of Carol. He admired her assertiveness in trying to get good programming for Darla and said that both parents had been very involved in getting the best for Darla. He elaborated:

> The Helms are caring parents who have good parenting skills. They have a lot to do, a lot of pressure and adjustment, and they've maintained a family environment through it all. It's impressive. The family is still together. They have perseverance. They care a great deal about Darla. I know a lot of families where one parent won't accept responsibility. I usually deal with just one parent. But at conferences it's

always James and Carol. James is generally more realistic, Carol more optimistic and idealistic. At case conferences they balanced each other well. They live in a trailer, but everything is well cared for. James owns his own machine shop. They are a hardworking couple. Any community would be glad to have the Helms.

Elise Yoder had been with the special education cooperative since Darla was 10, when she was first employed as an aide for Darla's class. Darla was her student for most of the 4 years preceding enrollment at the Clay Center, except for the last year when Darla was suspended and received homebound and "personalized," one-on-one school instruction. Even then, Darla frequently was integrated into Yoder's class. Yoder was the teacher that Darla scratched; nevertheless, Yoder generously described the attack as an "outburst of frustration" on Darla's part and not something that she did intentionally or maliciously. She sympathized with Darla, claiming that Darla had no other way of communicating her feelings. It had not been Yoder's decision to have Darla suspended. Apparently, when Quail and Ingalls heard of the attack they felt it was time to "take action." Yoder said that she had never really been afraid of Darla, but described herself as "wary." She knew that Darla had a tendency to strike out suddenly and unexpectedly.

Darla was fairly passive and independent when left alone, and Elise felt guilty about a tendency to "neglect her." The aides were afraid of Darla and did not like to work with her, so Darla mainly paced on the opposite side of the room from the rest of the class until Yoder had the opportunity to work with her. Darla's needs were very different from those of her peers, and because Darla did not like to be included in group activities, it was difficult to program for her. Elise had eight other students to worry about. In addition to lacking the time to program for Darla, Elise felt that she lacked the competencies and knowledge necessary for teaching a child with autism. Elise never felt that Darla was appropriately placed in her class.

After Darla left for the Clay Center, Elise neither saw nor spoke with Carol Helm. She said that she had considered calling, because she cared about both Darla and Carol, but she was reluctant to get involved. Carol sometimes told her more than she wanted to know. Elise sympathized with Carol, but was wary of forming a closer relationship. She felt that Carol might have greater communication and friendship needs than Yoder would want to meet. She herself was teaching full time and had a small daughter and felt that her time was over-committed already. She did not know James Helm as well as she knew his wife. He came to the important conferences, but had not been in as close or frequent contact with Elise as Carol had been. Carol perceived James as a caring father and a supportive husband.

The Clay Center

The turn off the highway for the Clay Center brings the driver into a very large public school campus of gray and brown one-story buildings. On a school day, the drive through this complex passes playgrounds with children of varying ages and ethnic origins, a few of whom are in wheelchairs. Classroom windows are vibrantly decorated. Plants, trees, and flowers are abundant on the school grounds. The road then winds past other classroom buildings for a short distance to a handsome and quite modern red brick complex of attached two-story town houses. This complex houses the administrative and residential parts of the Clay Center. Built more recently than the public school complex, the Clay Center also includes seven classrooms, which were added to the existing school buildings and constructed to conform to them.

The Clay Center for Research and Programming for Adolescents with Autism, as implied by its title (which, as noted earlier, is a pseudonym), has a dual research and programming mission and is designed to provide short-term intensive programming for students. The program staff, with families and local community providers, plan and experiment with programs that are eventually to be carried out in the student's home community.

The adolescent program in which Darla was enrolled was an education/ vocational program with recreational and community living components. One of eight students in the seven-day-a-week, year-round program, Darla lived in a group home with three other students. She had her own room, which best fit her needs as she had erratic sleep patterns and a need for her own personal space. The program had general goals for all eight students, which included learning functional life-long skills and behaviors, developing vocational skills and work habits, becoming independent in self-care and home-living skills, learning leisure activities, and developing useful communication and social interaction skills. Although students are initially assessed and are accepted for this transitional program only if they show the potential to benefit from Clay training, the range of characteristics of students admitted to the program is very broad. Thus, in addition to group goals, each student's program is highly individualized with specific goals and objectives.

Maintenance of a relationship between the family and the teenager with autism is a major goal of Clay Center staff. Students go home for a one- to two-week vacation six times a year, if possible. They can also go home on weekends between scheduled vacations. Parents are asked to write journals on issues of concern when their son or daughter is at home. Parent support group meetings are held for parents once a month on Sunday evenings. Additionally, parents are encouraged to observe and participate in the programming at the Clay Center. The social worker and other Clay staff members keep in frequent touch with parents over the telephone, and families are sent weekly journals from the group home, school, and recreation programs.

The professional staff in Darla's program included licensed specialists in education, speech pathology, health education, school psychology, therapeutic recreation, and adapted physical education. Because the Clay Center was affiliated with the university, the program was staffed by college students, many of whom were training to work with persons with developmental disabilities. These students were men and women from all parts of the world with an array of cultural and life experiences.

The Helms' Decision. In the spring before Darla's admission, Linda Morrow, the Clay Adolescent Program Coordinator, met with the Helms. At that meeting, James said he was concerned that someone might "take advantage" of Darla. He said that this had happened elsewhere, and he wanted a guarantee that it would not happen at the Clay Center. About 10 days before Darla was to arrive, Cindy McCormick, the Clay social worker, called the Helms to make final arrangements and reported that Carol was "hysterical," saying, "You'll do what everyone else has done!" She very emotionally expressed her concern about male supervisors in the group homes. Both Morrow and Clay's Associate Director, Sandra Werner, were called to the telephone to discuss Carol's concerns with her. Carol implied that Darla previously had been abused in a residential center and she worried that such an incident might recur.

On several occasions, Clay administrators explained to the Helms how they staffed the residential part of the program. They tried to reassure the Helms that staff members were well-trained and trusted by fellow workers and administrators. They also informed the Helms that they had the weekend to make up their minds about whether Darla would attend. If they had not decided by then, Darla's place at the center would not be held for her. At the specified deadline, Carol responded that Darla would be attending the Clay Center. By the time this contact was made, Mrs. Helm had calmed down (or as Werner said, she was less "hysterical") and even apologized about the emotional level of her previous call.

McCormick remembered feeling, "This woman is going to be awfully tough to deal with." She speculated that James had calmed Carol down and had talked her into letting Darla come to the Clay Center. When the family arrived at the center, Carol was tense and quiet. The social worker introduced Carol and James to other parents, and Carol started to chat with mothers of other students. Kelly Fincher, a home programmer, also made a point of introducing them to the female group home staff. When the Helms left Darla, they both seemed to be in a better mood. Ken Ingalls later confessed that he was surprised that the Helms ever consented to Darla living away from home since they had always been so protective of her.

At the time, Clay staff did not make any inferences about reasons behind the Helms' concerns. They assumed that sexual abuse was just a special anxiety of Carol's. The administrators had informed the residential staff of Carol's fears and had asked them to make some minor changes in dealing with showering and dressing routines. The staff had been asked to prepare a short statement that described portions of the program that involved any physical contact (e.g., back rubbing) with Darla. This had been given to the Helms for their signature upon Darla's arrival. It was anticipated that Carol would become alarmed each time the program included anything that could be construed as sexual, and the staff wanted Carol to know about the curriculum ahead of time. Carol mentioned a couple of incidents to Cindy McCormick, including the alleged abuse at the Mapleton center. Still, McCormick later confessed, she merely listened and waited for Carol to divert her attention from the sexual topic, which she felt was a particular "hang-up" of Carol's. It did not occur to McCormick—or perhaps she did not have the confidence— to discuss Darla's sexuality with Carol in more detail and depth. No one asked Carol to explain her concerns, and the only discussion about Darla's sexual behaviors prior to admission focused on Darla's parading around nude. A pregnancy test was not included as part of the initial physical examination.

Darla at the Clay Center. Darla has dark wavy hair and a pretty face and smile. Her walk is bouncy as if she is happy or excited. She is medium height, 5'4", and her weight varies from 130 to 145 pounds. Generally people at Clay liked Darla when they first met her, but when they tried to teach her or direct her, their attitudes changed. Darla's autism leads her not to trust people; she wants to do everything her own way, and she is frequently violently negative. She pushes people away, shoves them, turns her back and walks away, or shakes her head urgently and persistently. Sometimes she whines or screams —the word "no" is communicated, even if unspoken. When Darla wants something, she can plainly convey her meaning. She often seizes someone's hand and drags them to the object she desires, or she just grabs whatever she wants. Darla often hits herself, runs into objects, and flops down on hard surfaces. She rears back and bangs her head on objects when agitated. Such self-injurious behavior is common in individuals with autism. Less harmful but equally disturbing, Darla screams and moans, and paces back and forth, almost like a wind-up toy.

When Darla came to the Clay Center, she was 15, but her self-care skills were more like those of a 3-year-old. She wet herself almost every night and often during the day. Occasionally she had a bowel accident and was plagued with constipation alternating with diarrhea. At times she threw up, and it seemed to the staff that this vomiting followed episodes of overeating, or else was self-inflicted as part of her self-injurious, repetitive behavior pattern. Darla had pica and would eat anything, edible or not, and so the staff had to watch her carefully, in both the home and classroom setting. Darla also slept irregularly. She would awaken during the night or early in the morning and wander around.

Testing and assessment revealed objective data about Darla's competencies and behavior. Her IQ measured in the severe range of retardation, her social skills and communication skills were like those of a child between the ages of 9 to 18 months, while her ability to put together and take apart objects with several parts was well-developed. Darla especially liked working at small assembly-type tasks with both her hands and was good at fixing things, like putting the handle back on the door of a car or putting a clothes rack together. At times she would work for 45 minutes or more on repetitive assembly tasks. However, she might alter the task a bit or jump out of her seat for a quick pace around the room and then resume work. When motivated, Darla sometimes imitated what others did.

Like most people with autism, Darla performed best in a structured, individualized program. At the time of her entry into the Clay Center, Darla required a semi-isolated program designed to accommodate her special needs; the separate program not only benefited Darla, but was necessary to prevent her from interfering with her peers' progress.

Informal observations revealed that Darla could understand concrete one-step directions, but that it was virtually impossible to explain changes or tell her about future events. The design of a communication system for Darla was of primary importance. However, attempts to establish a combination of a communication board and sign language use for Darla were extremely slow, since she did not attend well to pictures. Because she liked to manipulate items, a velcro board was made for her with removable pictures of activities. She would be prompted to take the picture to the appropriate activity to facilitate association and then return it to the board. Using this method, she clearly associated pictures with activities and appeared to have potential for expansion. Progress was slow, however, because Darla required daily practice with the board, with multiple repetitions always applied to actual activities or situations. She seemed to know only that she should make some response. She did not distinguish hand signs when three or four were introduced. Her usual response was to go randomly through her repertoire or imitate a model, with no signs of comprehension. For communication, Darla began to use "eat" and "finish" signs, but continued to rely on pushing away gestures, pulling adults toward objects, or shaking her head as more typical and automatic means of communication.

The Clay Center program had a strong emphasis on community integration but this, too, was slow for Darla. Taking Darla into the community was always difficult. Once a routine was established, she became agitated by any change. She often became upset at the entry to a building, apparently reacting to the unknown people and stimuli around her. When agitated, Darla screamed, pinched, pulled hair, and tried to escape. The one community setting that Darla loved was the swimming pool at the Y-Center. There she seemed to relax and it was a positive place to instruct her.

DARLA'S PREGNANCY

Darla Helm had been at the Clay Center for adolescents with autism for 2 months when her pregnancy was noticed. Staff were gradually getting to know her. Careful records were kept on the students, including weight records. In spite of a low calorie diet, Darla's weekly weigh-ins revealed persistent weight increases. At a weekly staffing, the recreation programmer, Pam Brookshire, who helped Darla with showers and dressing at the Y-Center, cautiously noted that the weight gain seemed to be primarily in her breasts and abdomen. "She couldn't be pregnant," they discussed; it seemed unlikely given her close supervision. Nevertheless everyone at the staffing quickly concurred that Darla looked pregnant. A decision was made to administer a "home" pregnancy test at the Center the next morning.

When the Center nurse, Margie Jasper, found the test results to be positive, she asked Linda Morrow for direction. They decided to call the Student Health Center at the University with which the Clay Center is affiliated. The director there claimed that Darla was not eligible for their health care services. The next call was made to a local family planning agency. There a vaginal/pelvic examination confirmed the pregnancy, and the examining nurse, Fran Ellis, estimated that Darla was between 16 and 20 weeks pregnant.

Cindy McCormick and Linda Morrow made the next call, to Darla's father, to inform him of the pregnancy and the suspected length of gestation. McCormick then informed James that since Darla was a minor, the Clay Center staff would be obligated to report the pregnancy to the welfare department. After their call to James, they immediately notified the county welfare department in the city where the Clay Center is located, the State Department of Education responsible for placing Darla at the Clay Center, and the State Protection and Advocacy Director.

Without informing Clay Center staff that they were coming, that evening James and Carol came to take Darla home. The trip from their mobile home on the outskirts of Winthrop, in a rural area of the state, to the Clay Center is about 100 miles of winding, narrow roads.

A male home programmer, who was present when the Helms arrived, described what happened:

> I told them that Darla was in the shower with another staff member. James Helm looked angry but he did not say much. Carol Helm was crying and went right up to see Darla. She felt Darla's abdomen and kept asking the female residential program assistant who was present, "How long have you known? Are you sure?" They waited around to blow dry Darla's hair and pack her things and then they left. We felt uncomfortable and very sad. It was clear both parents were upset.

Reactions of the Medical Community

The first "outsider" to interact with Darla was Ellis, a registered nurse at the local family planning clinic. On November 8, Ellis received a telephone call from Clay staff and was told that they would be bringing a 15-year-old with autism, who was suspected of being pregnant, for an examination to confirm the pregnancy and get an estimate on its length. Ellis knew that people with autism often do not like being touched and she was concerned about how she would proceed in the examination. Ellis had worked with youngsters with disabilities, and even autistic youngsters. In the early 1960s she had spent a year at a psychiatric hospital and then 3 years at an outpatient clinic where she frequently had clients with disabilities. Working at the family planning clinic, Ellis had been exposed to many teenage pregnancies; however, she felt that working with a nonverbal pregnant girl was a particularly difficult challenge. She would be unable to get a medical or menstrual history or any information about the possible date of conception. Ellis would not be able to discuss the ramifications of the pregnancy, the support system, or Darla's plans for how to proceed—all things she would normally discuss with patients.

Ellis recalled meeting Darla and two Clay Center staff members at the door of the clinic. While she talked to staff about the case, she observed Darla go to the toy box in the waiting room, pick up a doll, shake it around a few times, and drop it back into the box. At the request of Clay staff Darla then passively accompanied Ellis to the examining room. Although she whimpered throughout the examination, she was cooperative about getting undressed, getting on the examination table, and being examined. There was no kicking or other physical aggression, as Ellis had feared, and so she did not feel personally threatened. Because Ellis knew that this was only an examination for pregnancy confirmation and determination of fetal age, and that Darla would not be continuing as a patient at the clinic, her examination was "not as com-

plete" as normal. Based on uterus palpitation and measurement, Ellis estimated that Darla was about 16 to 20 weeks into her pregnancy. Although local
clinics would not perform an abortion after a pregnancy was of 10 weeks'
duration, Ellis gave the Clay staff a list of clinics that would terminate pregnancies as advanced as Darla's. There were two clinics in adjacent states (each
approximately 3 hours away from Darla's hometown of Winthrop) that would
abort pregnancies of up to 22–24 weeks' gestation. Ellis knew that Darla would
not be able to make such a decision, but she assumed that Darla's parents
would decide to have the pregnancy terminated. Ellis also commented that
Darla's genitalia were expanded and did not resemble those of a virginal 15-
year-old but indicated a more sexually active teenager. She shared her suspicion that Darla's pregnancy was probably not the result of a one-time or first-
time experience. She told Clay staff to let the child abuse investigator know
about her findings.

The next medical stop during Darla's pregnancy was to her family doctor, Andrew Edge, on November 9. She was also seen by Yvonne Geneva,
the nurse in Edge's office. Geneva talked to the interviewer about Darla and
her family before Dr. Edge arrived at his office. Geneva had known the Helm
family for many years and had first met Darla when she was 5, at the time
Carol Helm switched Darla from their pediatrician, Anthony Wilder. Carol
had told Geneva that she was angry at Wilder for suggesting that Darla be
institutionalized. Geneva related that once Darla had taken two quarter-sized
knobs off adjustable lights in the waiting room, and these had never been
found. They assumed that Darla had eaten them. Since that time they had
always scheduled early appointments for Darla so that she could be examined as soon as she arrived. Geneva reported that physical examinations of
Darla were usually done by following Darla as she walked around the room,
although her behavior varied considerably from one appointment to the next.

Geneva had developed a personal relationship with Carol over the years.
She admired her caring relationship with Darla and felt sorry for her because
of her many burdens. Geneva said Carol often confided in her and relied on
her support in difficult situations. Geneva claimed that she and Carol had
both cried when Carol called to tell her the Clay staff's report of the pregnancy and to make an appointment with Edge. Geneva scheduled a pre-office-
hour appointment for Darla because she knew that Darla might "yell out"
and pace in the waiting room, which would upset other patients waiting there.

After Andrew Edge arrived, he and Geneva were interviewed together.
Geneva let Edge do most of the talking, although she occasionally interrupted
to clarify a point or to correct him. Andrew Edge had grown up in Winthrop
and had taken over his father's family practice a couple of years earlier. Geneva
had been the father's nurse prior to working with Andrew. During his 2 years
in practice, Edge had seen Darla about eight times because of earaches, rec-

tal protrusions (a condition in which rectal muscles lose their support and the rectum starts to come outside of the body), constipation, and skin lacerations. Once he had met Darla in the emergency room at the local hospital because she had eaten 10 Contact capsules. Edge had one other handicapped patient—a 25-year-old male with mental retardation; however, this man had no behavior problems and had verbal skills, and Edge felt comfortable with him.

Reactions of the Clay Center Staff

Although several staff members had been vaguely thinking about Darla in terms of her being "pregnant," she had been at the Clay Center 2 months before anyone seriously discussed pregnancy as a real possibility. Pam Brookshire, the recreation therapist, had taken Darla swimming and noticed when Darla was dressing that her naked shape looked very pregnant.

> It had occurred to me that Darla might be pregnant. Her weight gain was in her stomach and her breasts. I had a frightened feeling for Darla. I was disgusted that Darla had been in that situation and for what she had to go through. I went to the nurse about it.

After Brookshire's disclosure to Margie Jasper and Linda Morrow at the staffing, things happened very quickly. Morrow talked to her immediate supervisor, Sandra Werner, and filled her in on the reasons behind the decision to administer a home pregnancy test. Werner's first thought was, "We never asked about sex when Mrs. Helm got so upset about the male supervisors. Why didn't we think to give Darla a pregnancy test? The mom was trying to tell us and we didn't pick up on it." Although others perceived the situation differently, Werner felt deluged with concerns.

> I didn't know what to do. I felt uninformed about legal procedures. I was worried about staff morale. Staff were concerned, confused, angry, and burned out. We wanted to take Darla to the University Health Center. We called a nurse there, who called her superior. He refused to have her examined there. He said it was not their responsibility. I don't know why we didn't call our personal practitioners, but the family planning agency seemed the natural place to go. We discussed what to tell staff and decided who would call the Helms. We were determined that if the pregnancy had happened while Darla was enrolled at the Clay Center, we would maintain interdisciplinary networking at all times; that we would protect male staff members. We would have to have legal counseling. I heard that Mr. Helm was hos-

tile when called about the pregnancy, and I was afraid for staff
because of his anger. We kept the group home locked and got extra
staff to deal with James Helm if he became violent.

The Clay Center Director, Chuck Giesler, was notified that Darla was
showing symptoms of pregnancy and that there were plans to go to the local
family planning agency to verify it. Giesler wanted to make sure that male
staff were not involved. He recalled that Mrs. Helm had said she had problems with male home programmers and staff in other residential settings, and
he had been consulted about what to do about that at the time. His position
then was that the staffing patterns were appropriate. Now he hoped that her
fears had not been realized. Giesler appeared to be less bothered personally
and less afraid about the consequences for the Center, even if it turned out
that the pregnancy had happened while she was at the Clay Center, than many
of his employees. He was able to tell himself that something problematic like
this is always likely to happen, and he felt the perpetrator could be prosecuted
without implicating the rest of the Center staff. Nevertheless, Giesler was
relieved to hear that Darla became pregnant before she came to the program.

The announced pregnancy made an impression on everyone. Those
interviewed showed strong emotions immediately (e.g., "We were all depressed. It was a sad occasion"; "I started to cry. Everyone got quiet"; "I practically vomited when I heard, I was so upset"; "Everything started swimming
in our heads"; "I was totally shocked"). Nurhan Tokar "knew it couldn't be
clients—I know the autistic—that was the last to come to mind. I felt the
abuse was pretty sick, pretty twisted. Taking advantage of one of the kids was
not right. I was disgusted." A male residential program assistant explained
his feelings.

> I was placing her in a different category: someone who could not get
> pregnant. It did not occur to me that pregnancy was even a possibility
> for Darla. I thought, "Damn, she's got problems enough." It seemed
> like all the problems you could pile on anybody were on top of this
> one person. Staff talked about it for 3 straight days. We clung to each
> other. We gritted our teeth. Some made black and white cases out of
> it. We argued about abortion. We were confused about who was in a
> position to make decisions about the situation.

Those interviewed many months later had vivid recollections of how they
heard the news. Teresa Bellows recalled:

> I remember exactly when I heard about it. Jerry Roderick, the speech
> therapist, came from a staffing and announced it. I was really just

shocked. I was in with the children. I happened to be working with
Darla. I was totally shocked. We knew she was gaining weight, but it
never crossed my mind that she could be pregnant. If she had been a
normal teenager I wouldn't have been surprised. I was very angry.
The profile fit. There was no question about pregnancy. We should
have known all along. I just didn't associate pregnancy with this population. Every minute of the day is regulated, coached, trained, supervised. If it had happened here there would have been a lawsuit,
people's jobs would be on the line, newspapers would get hold of it,
people would take their children out of the program.

Some Clay employees said they had suspected Darla's pregnancy before
it was announced. Bill Peterson said:

I was beginning to have a suspicion that Darla might be pregnant
shortly before I heard the news, so I wasn't particularly surprised.
The symptoms added up to pregnancy. The pregnancy explained
things: the frequent urination, the illnesses had been morning sick-
ness, the fact that her bras were too small, she'd be doing fine, then
get uncomfortable and she'd hit her stomach and scream. All the
symptoms, combined with the parental concern, added up to pregnancy. I had a strong hunch before the EPT was positive.

The immediate concern was that a Clay Center employee might be
responsible. A female recreation assistant said, "I thought someone at Clay
would get nailed." Kelly Fincher, a home programmer, said, "I was worried
that it had happened here and I asked myself, 'How do we screen employees?' I don't think that we screen them adequately, but I did have confidence
in our present staff." A male residential program assistant said, "It made me
realize that rape can happen with developmentally disabled people—they can
be taken advantage of. Staff here could potentially do such a thing. It's hard
to know staff well enough to say that nobody could have done it."

Nurhan Tokar had not been at the meeting when Darla's pregnancy was
announced, but he got a call from a co-worker who wanted to warn him about
it. He was upset because, as night supervisor in Darla's group home, he was
the one who was in the best position to have abused Darla, and he thought
that others would suspect him. He went through a traumatic time.

I was aware of my personal situation. Everyone tries to put it together. I was in the most vulnerable situation. I had the sense that
other staff were looking for indications to verify their suspicions of me
because I was a male who happened to be on duty at night. It was

bullshit that chance ended up to reflect on me. I don't see other staff much. I don't know many well because I work the night shift. I went to the program coordinator and told her that I didn't want to go to the meeting that was scheduled because I couldn't face everyone who was suspicious. I had taken extra precautions not to get myself in a precarious position because I was aware of the parents' concerns about male night supervisors. I had the female morning staff help her with dressing. I'm usually in a position to help the students dress, but I made sure that this was not the case with Darla. For a while everyone avoided interaction; they suspected someone in the system.

It was a great relief to Tokar, and others who considered themselves to be in a vulnerable position, to have the duration of the pregnancy established so promptly. Fortunately, the determination that Darla was 16–20 weeks pregnant was made the same day that her pregnancy was discovered, so there was only a period of a few hours when Clay staff worried about the possibility that impregnation happened while Darla was at the Center. Jerry Roderick said, "There was relief at finding that it did not happen here—a load off male staff's minds, especially the male night supervisors." Linda Morrow speculated: "We all could have been implicated if she had been pregnant a shorter period of time."

Cindy McCormick was angry at the Helms for insinuating that Darla might have been abused at the Clay Center, when she was already pregnant upon arrival. It occurred to McCormick that they might have been aware of Darla's condition and were trying to "pin something" on Center staff. McCormick had to "break the news" to the parents. She debated with her colleagues about which parent to call. When they decided on Carol, she was called but was not at home. McCormick then telephoned James at work. Linda Morrow was on another phone, both to document the reaction and, if necessary, to support her colleague. When James Helm was told that Darla was pregnant, it seemed to McCormick and Morrow that he was not overly shocked by the news. Morrow said: "Any parent would immediately be upset. He seemed to have no emotion. I thought that he would fall apart, cry, or have a strong reaction, but there was no response at the end of the line. James simply said, 'Thank you for calling.'" McCormick observed: "I found it odd that James was so cool. He said, 'Don't tell Carol. She won't be able to handle it.'" When McCormick told James that it appeared that Darla became pregnant before she arrived at the Clay Center, James denied it, but McCormick sensed that he might have an idea of how Darla got pregnant. She asked him if he knew when Darla had her last period, and he replied that Carol kept records, but he thought that it was during her last visit home.

A male residential assistant, who was present when the Helms came for

Darla, described his impressions: "They were obviously upset. His lips were close together. She was crying. I felt sorry for her. I had mixed feelings about him. I wasn't sure he hadn't raped Darla, so I wanted to hate him. I kept the interaction to a minimum." Lisa McNeil, who was also there, recalled thinking:

> The mother is a good person. She tries hard and wants the best for her daughter. I admire that she tries to implement the Clay Center methods at home. I feel sorry for the mom. I hope she doesn't know more than she is saying. I met the parents one other time, in October when they brought Darla back after vacation. The mom took abuse from Darla. Darla went right up to her to pinch her. To see a kid do that to her mom was hard to take.

McNeil had worried about how the Helms would act and was relieved when they departed.

In retrospect, several staff members were puzzled that no one had picked up on the clues pointing to pregnancy or that they had not directly asked Carol Helm about the reasons behind her concerns about sexual abuse. The multidisciplinary staff routinely asks parents a number of questions about eating, sleeping, communication, self-care, and social interaction patterns, but they don't ask about sexual activities and behaviors, with the exception of masturbation. Kelly Fincher was puzzled that even after she had observed considerable sexual interest on Darla's part, she still did not ask the Helms about their perceptions of Darla's sexuality. In fact, when the Helms brought Darla back after her first home visit in September, James confronted a male residential employee about sexually provocative behaviors that he had not observed before, such as rubbing against his legs. Feeling on the defensive when faced with such loaded questions, this employee did not ask the Helms questions, but tried to calmly assure them that the Clay Center was a safe place for Darla.

Darla's Program During the Pregnancy

Both the Helms and the Winthrop school officials were determined to have Darla continue at the Clay Center in spite of her pregnancy. Although Quail was proud that during his tenure as Winthrop Superintendent pregnant adolescents had been allowed to remain in school and a high school-based, daycare program had been started, he worried about Darla's coming back. Quail argued that he had no faculty who were adequately trained to educate an autistic teenager, especially one who was pregnant. Quail understood the rationale behind Clay staff's worries about the special liabilities that Darla's pregnant state presented, but argued that his system would be in the same position. School board members were kept informed about Darla's situation, and they counseled Quail to fight to keep her at the Clay Center.

Clay administrators were anxious about Darla's return. According to Chuck Giesler, the Clay Center Director:

> I was worried about the environment that Darla was in and about the safety of her and her unborn. I never had the feeling that she had to go home, but I wanted precautions. It was my idea to contact Bob Birmingham, the university lawyer, about making a contract to protect the staff from potential liabilities regarding Darla's pregnancy. She had the right to an education, and it had already been decided that we were the appropriate program. So there was never any question in my mind that she should return, pregnant or not; however, I wanted to protect Darla and my staff.

Sandra Werner recalled her stand:

> She was our responsibility and so she needed to come back, but I was concerned about staff's reaction. We felt that we would have hostility from staff if we decided to take her back. Those were bad days. We felt like we were just keeping a lid on the situation. I felt an undercurrent of concern, resentment. I felt that we were getting in over our heads. I looked for an answer in the literature—that's the solution for those of us in the Ivory Tower—to look to the literature. I found nothing. We had to keep her in the program to protect Darla, but at a big cost. Yet it was a cost we had to bear. We talked at length about whether Darla should come back. Chuck Giesler, Linda Morrow, and I decided that we would make the decision. I felt that staff was thinking, "You're making a decision, but you're not with Darla." It was like a general sending the battalions out to war. You stay back and send them off to battle; let them take the risks. Since we run the program with an interdisciplinary philosophy, we usually make decisions based on majority consensus. However, this time we felt we should make the decision and we concluded that she should come back. The state had given us authority and we could provide a program. I felt that the local system had washed their hands of the case. If she did not come back here they would not do anything. I felt ambivalent. I did not really feel secure that we were doing the right thing. We felt that we needed a system to protect everyone involved. Bob Birmingham drew up a contract to cover all possibilities. We wanted assurances—a contract to protect everyone. Plus, we wanted to make sure that everyone did their part—welfare, the Helms. All parents signed contracts when

their children were enrolled at the Clay Center, but we had to
develop a special contract with conditions for liabilities more appropriate for serving a pregnant client.

Others remembered that Sandra Werner was opposed to Darla's remaining
at the Clay Center because of potential risks and the possibility of being held
liable for mishaps. In contrast to Werner, Linda Morrow believed that staff
appreciated the administration's efforts in making appropriate decisions and
in supporting direct contact staff's concerns. She worked closely with the classroom, recreation, and residential employees and listened to their opinions
on a daily basis. Because of these close relationships, Morrow believed that
her staff felt they had been represented in the decision-making process on
issues within their responsibility.

Bob Birmingham and Linda Morrow worked late for several nights, with
frequent phone calls to Fred Quail. Finally, on the Tuesday before Thanks-
giving, Birmingham, Morrow, Werner, Giesler, Ingalls, and Quail met at the
Clay Center to review the complex contract. Ingalls then took the contract to
the Helms, who had to sign before Darla could return.

Darla was re-enrolled in the Clay Center 23 days after the pregnancy
was discovered. Morrow and McCormick, who had both made an early commitment to accommodating Darla's special needs during her pregnancy, recognized that the Clay Center staff would need additional training and special
support during this stressful period. They were determined to put forth the
extra effort to provide this effectively. McCormick and Morrow also felt
obligated to follow up on their sexual abuse report, so they made a number
of calls to state officials to gather information on how to prod Winthrop
authorities into making more investigations and possibly taking legal action
in the case. They felt that the state laws and system were not responsive to
Darla's needs. Although they were suspicious of the parents' role in the abuse,
they tried not to let their personal feelings interfere with the support they
provided the family. They felt that the Helms should be encouraged to make
responsible decisions about abortion, tubal ligation, and custody of the baby.
Another part of facilitating good care for Darla was frequent interaction with
community professionals who provided services.

Bill Peterson felt he had to rethink the classroom program in order to
meet Darla's needs during her pregnancy.

When the parents made the decision for Darla to have the baby, then
we had an educational problem to deal with. We had been pressuring
Darla to adjust to routines. Now her physical needs and well-being
had to take priority over educational concerns. We formally wrote up
a program that would reduce demands and allow Darla more time to

rest. This strategy helped diminish some of the negative behaviors we were seeing. She walked around the room smiling, for a change. Positive affect increased. She touched nicely [i.e., instead of pinching or pulling hair], and she was more at ease in the program even though she had physical distress with the pregnancy. But she was always inconsistent and we had a difficult time. Some felt that she shouldn't be in the program. Others felt that she was making excellent progress. There was conflict in the staff. Safety was a concern. I felt she would be just as safe here as at home and I thought she could continue to make gains in the program, but others were worried that something would go wrong while they were in charge. I was not so worried about personal responsibility, because of the contract, but I felt that we did have to watch her extremely closely and that was a strain.

In spite of having additional medical responsibilities related to Darla's pregnant condition, Margie Jasper was in favor of her return to the Center. Jasper saw Darla once a week during the pregnancy and weighed her, checked her blood pressure, checked her urine for infection, and monitored her diet. Jasper provided staff with in-service sessions on delivery and postnatal infant care, and made arrangements with the ambulance company and the local hospital in case Darla went into labor prematurely while still at the Clay Center.

Pam Brookshire had to modify the recreational program considerably to accommodate a pregnant student, yet said:

I really felt bad for Darla. She couldn't understand what was happening to her. I thought of her sitting in the trailer at home and I wondered if we would ever get her back. I also worried that nothing was being done to stop the abuse. I was concerned about decisions that the Helms were making that I had no role in. I felt Darla deserved to come back. It wasn't her fault that she had gotten pregnant. I felt that she had made progress. She had not been here long enough to say that she did not fit in. But I was concerned about the medical issues involved. I knew I had to change her programming—Darla could not be "displayed" on stage in the community. I had to relocate her swimming from the Y to a private pool. I required more staff because I had to provide programming for her at Clay while I took the others into the community. It would not be fair to the other clients to keep them all at Clay because of Darla. I was also worried about my staff's ability to deal with a pregnant woman. We might not recognize her water breaking, because she often urinates in her pants. I preferred to have someone with medical knowledge with her all the time. I felt better when I learned that she would leave the center in February, a month before she was expected to go into labor.

Of Clay staff, residential workers were most opposed to Darla's remaining at the Center. As one said:

> I worried most about aggression by others and that her self-injurious behaviors might hurt the baby. We felt we could do a good job of caring for Darla, but we worried about the chance that something might happen. As a staff person you can't be everywhere. We worried about the stairs and the tub. Nobody really took a stand against her coming back but we let our concerns be known. We discussed the logistics of setting the situation up so that it would be as safe as possible for Darla with the least disruption for others.

Kelly Fincher said, "I really worried about premature labor. I wondered how we'd know she was in labor. I thought the baby might be born before we knew about it. It was a really anxious time. Even though the nurse gave us training, I worried all the time." Nurhan Tokar, who opposed having Darla back, said:

> Pregnant women go through changes of mood. I worried that she would wake up and scream and wake others, that she would disrupt the sleep patterns of others. Autistic kids often have sleep problems anyway. We were having problems with Robert. The whole group home would be like a monkey ranch and I did not know if I could deal with it. I'm alone in the group home at night. I remembered talking about her being better off at home. I had delivered my two children at home myself with the help of a midwife; and so I didn't feel too concerned about an emergency birth, but I joked with the others that it would happen during my alternate's shift and I knew he could not handle it. Personally I did not want to have a pregnant woman in that environment. Our kids have no remorse. If they hit someone, they have no guilty conscience. I feared possible aggression from the other clients. They would not understand that she was pregnant and needed special care. I hoped that she would leave for the time she was pregnant. Retrospectively I feel that my fears were not justified.

Lisa McNeil said:

> I wanted her back and I was willing to have her in my group home, but I needed a break and it was nice to know that we did not have to have her back if the legal ramifications couldn't be controlled or if we

felt that we could not meet her needs. I knew that a lot of her behaviors were because of the pregnancy. A number of nights I went home hating the kid, feeling burned out, hating myself; I felt I could do nothing to please her. Putting her on a special diet put pressure on staff. Around February I was worried that she would have the baby. We had a procedure for early labor, for the birth, but I worried about cutting the umbilical cord. The nurse said to restrain Darla, but that would not be easy. We knew we were legally protected unless we were blatantly careless with Darla, but we did not want to botch up anyway. It was a stressful time.

Most admitted to a great relief when, 4 weeks before the scheduled delivery, Darla went home on maternity leave.

DARLA'S SEXUALITY

Because of her pregnancy, it was obvious that Darla had engaged in sexual intercourse. There was little consensus, however, about whether the impregnation resulted from coercion or willing cooperation. In fact, the range of opinions about her physical appearance and her interest in sex was great. It was also clear that participants' attitudes toward disability and sexuality were woven into perceptions of Darla.

Physical Appearance

Clay Center staff and community professionals gave varied impressions of Darla's physical appearance; some felt she "looked normal." Giesler said, "She looks like any normal young lady, a typical 15-year-old. She looks like a junior or senior high school student." Nurhan Tokar said: "Put a cigarette in her mouth, a leather jacket on her, and put her in front of a high school—she'd look like an average high school kid with a bad attitude. She doesn't look handicapped, but she doesn't seem happy. She's mostly frowning or screaming." Ken Ingalls said, "She's very athletic looking. She's strong. She can really run fast. If she weren't autistic she'd be the star female athlete in Winthrop."

Many described Darla as "pretty" or "physically attractive," remarking on her "pretty eyes" or "nice complexion." Others "could not understand" how Darla could be thought attractive. Usually, these people focused on what they felt to be obvious signs of autism. One judged, "She's too autistic-looking to be pretty." Another remarked, "I can't believe people think she's pretty; I look at her and think handicapped, autistic, retarded." Darla was described as "vacant-looking" by another. Some felt she could compete with nonhandicapped teenagers in attractiveness, whereas others felt her "handicapped" appearance made her physically, and especially sexually, unattractive.

Observations of Sexual Behavior

Almost all of the Clay staff who worked directly with Darla had observed some type of sexual behavior on her part. As Brookshire declared, "It is obvious that she has sex drive." Parley said, "At first I had a hard time trying to imagine that she'd had sex, but, because of a number of things she does, I could see that she'd probably had experience." Felicia Tudor gave a vivid account of an observation.

> One day she lay on the waterbed, sprawling sexually and moving rhythmically—it was obvious she enjoyed a sexual feeling—she was ecstatic. She's a sexual person who, I guess, has learned to enjoy sexual relationships. But I don't think sex is related to a special feeling of attachment to another person.

Some felt that Darla's sexual behaviors were fairly similar to those of other clients, perhaps differing in degree but not kind. As Teresa Bellows related:

> In terms of sexuality she was not really different. She did things other students do. She masturbated frequently, but at the time I didn't think it was because of her previous sexual experiences. Looking back, her relationship with male staff pointed to previous heterosexual involvement.

Brookshire said: "We addressed Darla's public masturbation problem, which we were trying to redirect to the appropriate private place. We always train clients that masturbation is private and they're to go to their room for that."

Others felt that her sexual behaviors were unique. Peterson judged Darla's behaviors to be atypical, but cautioned that his awareness of parental concerns about sex may have caused him to look for signs of unusual behavior. Roderick said, "She was displaying sexual behaviors not typical of a 15-year-old, particularly an autistic 15-year-old." Fincher recalled:

> I began to wonder if she had sexual experience. First, she masturbated so much. All the kids come from restrictive backgrounds in terms of masturbation. It was unusual that she came from a home environment where she'd learned to do it so much. I thought that odd.

Most had observed Darla masturbate with objects, which they said other clients usually did not do—others masturbated manually or rubbed against furniture or other large stationary objects. Darla rubbed against chairs and tables, but nobody had observed her masturbate with her hands and no one had seen her reach orgasm during masturbation. Tokar summarized, "Darla always used off-the-wall objects for masturbation." Darla had been observed to use balls, cushions, a plastic horse, a Kermit the Frog doll, and a large, ball-shaped light plastic chair for masturbation. In the group home her favorite object for masturbation was a 16–18-inch-long wooden boat. She mainly rubbed her external genitalia with objects and had not been observed to insert them into her vagina. She usually rubbed the objects through her clothing, although she had been observed to push objects beneath her clothes to masturbate.

Winthrop special education teacher Elise Yoder said that Darla had always masturbated with objects and had selected favorite objects in the classroom, which she consistently used. According to Yoder, Darla would always stop when requested to; thus, public masturbation was not a big problem while Darla was in her class. Peterson also felt that Darla's masturbation, though frequent, did not interfere with her school program.

> We saw stimulation with objects. I saw her flop, face down, on the couch and stick a plastic horse between her legs. We saw maybe a little more sexual behavior than with others. Other students had learned that masturbation was private. (Or, maybe I'm a little desensitized to the others' masturbation. They've been here longer than Darla.) It didn't seem unusual to see more open masturbation with Darla. She masturbated frequently, but only when disengaged. She did it when she was tired, during free time, or in the afternoon when the program is not as structured.

Clay employees said that telling Darla to stop or redirecting her to another activity was successful in stopping masturbation.

Vulnerability to Abuse

Some felt that Darla, unlike many other adolescents with severe mental retardation, was physically attractive—therefore men would be interested in having sexual interaction with her. Most felt that Darla was especially vulnerable to sexual abuse mainly because she was nonverbal and would be unable to name her abuser. Lisa McNeil said, "If Darla were being raped, nobody—the neighbors or anyone—would notice anything strange because she screams and cries all the time." Others hypothesized that because Darla was so strong and could be so aggressive, and because she avoids strangers, she might not be very susceptible to abuse by strangers. Dr. Jones, a gynecologist, marveled that she had let anyone close enough to her for her to get pregnant. Similarly, Laidlaw, the family's lawyer, said, "She can't protect herself; well, on second thought, I guess that's only true to a certain extent, but she can't understand the consequences of sexual intercourse." Sandra Werner elaborated:

> I'm not really comfortable with Darla's situation. I'm not optimistic that she's not going to be raped again. I struggle with what brings Darla pleasure. Darla may need sex, but how to provide it becomes a big question. People will take advantage of her. Darla could have initiated the sex—this may be a result of her behavior. We have to ask, "What is rape?" Then I worry that I'm falling into the "women who get raped bring it upon themselves" trap. If a woman initiates sex, where does the responsibility fall? Darla can't take responsibility for her behavior. What does that suggest for the other person?

Carol had confided to Cindy McCormick that she was afraid that Darla was vulnerable to sexual molestation. The Helms were so worried about others taking sexual advantage of Darla that they had confronted Clay administrators about her being alone with male staff. At a November case conference in Winthrop, a few weeks after Darla's pregnancy was discovered, James angrily announced: "I want to find whoever did this to Darla . . . then I'll take my gun . . ."; and then went on to state that someone had "gotten at Darla" a couple of years before and was "doing time."

Elise Yoder recalled Carol's account of a sexual abuse incident that had happened the summer when Darla was 13. Carol had sworn Yoder to secrecy and then had a "pouring out." Carol said that someone in the neighborhood had probably raped Darla. Darla was supposed to have been in the yard, but disappeared. They eventually found her coming out of the man's house. Carol said this man had been involved in other abuse cases, for which he had been taken to court and was to "serve time." It was Elise's impression that the man no longer lived near the Helms and that he might be in prison. Carol never mentioned the case again, and Elise had heard nothing more about it, although the court news was printed in the local newspaper. In spite of being told about these incidents, Elise said that she would not accuse Carol of being "overly concerned" about sex and felt that Carol's fears were realistic and rational. In contrast, most Clay Center staff categorized Carol's concerns about sex as irrational.

Social/Sexual Interaction

When asked about Darla's sexual behaviors, only Brad Parley categorized her behavior as deliberately seductive. Parley had read the report that her parents did not want her around males. After watching her, he felt he knew why: Darla was seductive. Others thought that her physical attractiveness might result in men seeing her as a "sex object," but most felt that she did not consciously work on such an image for herself. However, many had observed Darla make physical advances of a sexual nature toward others. Darla generally showed little interest in the other clients at the Clay Center; nevertheless, she had been observed to initiate sexual-type contact with them on several occasions. Bellows had observed Darla pull Toni (female) on top of her when they were on the trampoline. Tudor had seen Darla pull Lindsay's (female) head toward her crotch. Fincher remembered that when Darla first arrived they "could not keep her off Lindsay." Darla continually went up to Lindsay to check underneath her underwear and inspect her genitalia. Staff interpreted this as Darla's attempt to figure out if Lindsay was male or female. For the most part, Darla ignored other clients even though they were "quite available." As Bellows said, "She had opportunity for sexual interaction with others. Robert masturbated 90% of the time for a while. She never approached him or took advantage of that." McNeil watched Darla walk naked into Tim's room after her shower. Tim was masturbating and Darla stood and watched. McNeil redirected her, saying, "This is Tim's private time. It is out-of-bounds." Darla left, as she was directed to, but returned to stand and watch again. She made no move toward him and, again, left when told to do so by staff.

At first Darla also avoided staff. Tokar said: "She was new and didn't know what to expect. These kids are inclined not to want any part of you for a while. She hadn't established trust with anyone." She gradually did form attachments to staff. As she got to know and trust staff she allowed them to come more into her space, to get physically closer to her. She liked to have her back or feet rubbed in the group home at night. In the final months of her pregnancy, staff rubbed her abdomen with lotion after showers because she had dry skin problems. She tolerated and appeared to enjoy this touching.

Several Clay staff reported that Darla had approached them sexually. A male home programmer said that Darla often came up to him and took his arms and wrapped them around her. A few Clay employees, both male and female, claimed that when Darla hugged she occasionally rubbed her pelvic area against them, but Bellows observed that Darla "mainly pressed her body against men—not women. She realized they were men. She hugged men differently." Similarly, Roderick said, "It's clear that she wants contacts with men. With females she just doesn't act the same." Peterson described Darla with Jerry Roderick.

Once Darla went and sat on Jerry's lap. She rubbed up against him. It was clear she wanted something sexual. I'm not sure "initiate" is the right word—enjoy either—but she might not have an adverse reaction to a sexual advance from someone else. Jerry was surprised and embarrassed. I could tell from that incident that a person might not need to use force to have sex with her. She went after Jerry. I heard that when she was being checked to determine if she was pregnant, she gave no resistance to a vaginal exam by the nurse. It seems that she does not mind having her genitals handled. Often Darla will initiate contact, that is, hugs. At other times she can be real aggressive when we initiate a hug if she isn't interested. One-fourth of the time she has an aggressive reaction to hugs. Sometimes she initiates contact, then for some reason pushes away.

Roderick also mentioned the incident: "As I was leaning back while sitting on the couch, Darla came over and straddled me in the genital area and she rocked back and forth. I was surprised. My initial reaction was 'someone doesn't learn this on their own.'" Still he was as "shocked and appalled" as the others when he learned that Darla was pregnant. McNeil had observed Darla sit astride a male staff member and move as he was lying on the floor watching television in the group home. She concluded: "I knew Darla had done it before and it had given her pleasure. I first thought 'what a terrible experience for her' and then I realized that it may have been a positive one that she was trying to repeat."

Another residential worker said that Darla had pulled staff members of both sexes down on top of her, especially after she had just showered. Her interpretation was that Darla was exhibiting "learned behavior." Another said, "Darla would pull you onto her and take your hands to her genitals, but she didn't protest when you stopped her." There were a couple of reports that Darla had attempted to pull people's faces toward her genitals.

Darla often wrapped her legs around male staff—usually when in the swimming pool at the Y. A male recreation assistant called this "stimulating herself." He would redirect her by attempting to focus her attention on another activity, but she would usually repeat her behavior. One employee called this "masturbating with men's legs" and remarked that "it is strange that she generally doesn't want to be around people but then uses them for masturbation."

Those who had observed Darla initiate sexual contact were less inclined to say that her pregnancy was the result of "rape" in the sense of "force having been used to make someone have sexual intercourse." Lisa McNeil said:

If she enjoys intercourse it puts a whole different light on this situation. I can see her as a willing participant. I think I can see her as an

aggressor in sex. But if she hadn't had previous knowledge of intercourse, she couldn't initiate it. Someone taught her how and they
shouldn't have. As sexually active as Darla appears to be, she may
have enjoyed the sex that got her pregnant. I wondered how abusive
the sex was for her. Technically, it was abuse because she was
under 16.

Tokar denied the possibility of Darla's being interested in sex or of initiating
sexual intercourse: "She can't be interested—she's autistic. She doesn't talk.
She functions like a 2-year-old. Masturbation does not indicate that she wants
it." In contrast, Donna Karnes, the Winthrop social worker, stated: "Hormones
still flow in autistic people. Things feel good anyway." Several staff members
expressed confusion about whether initiating sex, or responding favorably to
another's advances, constituted a form of "consent" in a nonverbal person.

CHAPTER 4

Jason's Birth

The discovery of Darla's pregnancy precipitated an eventful 4 months for Darla and her parents. The Helms had to secure appropriate medical care for their daughter as well as make plans for her offspring. Just as in the past, their roles as parents of a child with severe disabilities required patience, ingenuity, and stamina.

SEEKING PRENATAL CARE

The search for an obstetrician was Carol's first challenge. The Helms wanted Darla to have her baby close to home, rather than in the city where the Clay Center is located. The day after Carol and James took Darla home from the Clay Center, they had Dr. Edge examine her so that he could confirm the pregnancy. By listening to the fetal heartbeat and measuring Darla's abdomen with a sonometer, Edge estimated that midsummer was the date of conception. Edge did not do a vaginal exam because he felt that the initial exam would be difficult and that he was not even sufficiently staffed for doing the bloodwork that Darla would need to have done. The Helms brought up abortion, but apparently Edge informed them that a second trimester abortion was not only illegal in the state, but very dangerous, even life-threatening, and he would not recommend it. The Helms asked Edge to provide Darla with prenatal care and deliver the baby, but he refused on the grounds that he was a general practitioner—not an OB/GYN—and also because he practiced alone. Moreover, Edge felt Darla should have a Caesarean section, which he was not sure he could handle. During his short time in practice, Edge had had experience with a few other pregnant teenagers and had delivered a number of babies, but he did not feel competent in providing such services for Darla.

Edge referred the Helms to an acquaintance of his, Dr. Sheridan, whose office was in St. Teresa's Hospital in Mapleton. One visit from Carol and Darla apparently convinced Sheridan that he wanted nothing more to do with the case. Furthermore, he had "no ideas" about whom they could turn to for care. He was one of three individuals who reported the case to the Hudson County Child Protection Office.

In desperation, Carol turned to the Yellow Pages. She made approximately 15 to 20 calls to local clinics, OB/GYNs, and hospitals and explained Darla's situation. Her requests for help in locating services produced nothing. Finally, a Dr. Franklin seemed willing to listen. Distraught and tearful, Carol launched into a detailed account of her unsuccessful search for medical care. She pleaded with him over the telephone, telling him of her urgent need to find medical services for her daughter. Although he initially refused, eventually Franklin hesitantly consented to see Darla and scheduled an appointment for her. Like Dr. Edge, Franklin practiced alone and felt that two doctors working in partnership would be better equipped to deal with an adolescent with autism.

When Dr. Franklin was interviewed several months later, he admitted his reluctance to take the case because he knew "the problems would outweigh the rewards," but he agreed to treat Darla because he felt "morally obligated to treat a patient in need." He was unsure if anyone had referred the case to him, but remembered that in early December he received a call from Carol Helm, who was frustrated and upset with "the other gynecologists." Franklin said that sympathy for Carol's dilemma swayed him in his decision to handle the case. Thomas Franklin had a clear sense of medical ethics but was well aware of his shortcomings in being prepared to treat Darla. He was acutely cognizant of his vulnerability in a world of malpractice lawsuits, yet he felt professionally obligated to serve Darla in spite of personal fears and misgivings.

Dr. Franklin could recall nothing in his medical training that prepared him for this unique case and had little personal experience with people with disabilities; therefore he set about informing himself so he could appropriately treat Darla. He researched the medical literature for relevant information. He consulted with numerous colleagues, among whom was a physician friend who had a 22-year-old son with autism. This son was not as severely retarded as Darla and had more communication skills; however, Franklin felt he learned a great deal from their conversations.

Franklin's first experience with Darla was hearing her scream in his reception room, where a number of other patients were also waiting for appointments. When he went to check about what was happening, he discovered Darla banging her head quite ferociously on the wall. Carol and Dot, Darla's maternal grandmother, were trying to calm and subdue Darla but were having little success. The other patients looked on with alarm, and although Franklin confessed to renewed feelings of inadequacy in treating Darla and wanting desperately to refuse to take her on, again compassion provided the incentive to continue the case.

Franklin readily got permission from other patients to take Darla ahead of schedule. During the examination Carol and Dot tried to "smother" Darla and divert her attention from the doctor; still Darla kicked and pulled away. He feared for his own physical safety as well as that of the patient. Franklin worried that Darla would fall off the examining table and injure herself or the baby. Again, the fear of lawsuits consumed his thoughts. At this point, Franklin decided that although he would continue to treat her he would not schedule subsequent prenatal examinations with the same frequency as he did for other patients. This decision was motivated not just by the desire to avoid future confrontations, such as occurred during this first examination, but also because Darla seemed to be a "very healthy young woman." He quickly learned to schedule Darla at a time when other patients were not present.

PREPARATIONS FOR THE BIRTH

Dr. Franklin decided that a Caesarean section would be the best method of delivery and scheduled the surgery for March 25. Dr. Hanes, an obstetrician in the city where the Clay Center is located, agreed to care for Darla if she should go into early labor while she was still at the Clay Center. Hanes's plans were to attempt to deliver the baby vaginally. Even though nobody at the Clay Center was involved directly in making decisions about the birthing process, Sandra Werner did some research and communicated her findings to the Helms.

> I questioned whether the C-section was in Darla's best interest. I asked a nursing instructor friend about all the risks and the pros and cons. I wanted our social worker to share that information with Carol and James; to provide them with information as we had been doing all along. The parents still wanted a C-section. We began to plan for a staffing at the local hospital. I really didn't think she'd go full-term. I was concerned about Darla's survival—there was a chance she might not come through it. I couldn't imagine Darla going through the delivery.

Although Franklin usually delivers babies at St. Teresa's, he scheduled Darla's C-section at Mapleton Southside Hospital because she was to have a tubal ligation, and sterilization surgery was not allowed at St. Teresa's. He informed Mapleton hospital staff about the nature of his patient and discussed the preparations for her care with them. Although he knew they had no choice but to provide for her, he still felt guilty about imposing on them. Franklin knew Darla would require an unusual amount of attention and care.

Margie Jasper and Cindy McCormick, the Clay Center nurse and social worker, talked to Dr. Franklin about the birth on March 11, approximately 2 weeks before Darla's surgery was scheduled. The two of them and Bill Peterson, the classroom teacher, went to Southside Hospital to provide an in-service session for hospital staff who were to work with Darla. They showed videotapes, discussed management strategies for dealing with Darla, and made arrangements for Darla's hospital stay. Later, questioning the benefits of their actions, Peterson confided that he thought there was a very negative tone to the training and the result was that hospital staff were more anxious and cautious about caring for Darla than they needed to be. Among the decisions that came out of the session were putting Darla on the pediatrics ward, requiring two family members or Clay staff members to be present in Darla's room around the clock, and keeping Darla in restraints whenever sufficient staff was not present to control her behavior. Franklin also planned to increase her dosage of sedatives.

AT THE HOSPITAL

On Sunday night, March 24, Darla was admitted to Mapleton Southside Hospital in preparation for the next day's delivery of her baby. Linda Morrow, Teresa Bellows, and Cindy McCormick went to the hospital, which was a 3-½ hour drive from the Clay Center. They had volunteered to spend the first 2 days of Darla's hospital stay with her. The three women, two of them mothers themselves and the third pregnant with her first child, kept records of the sequence of events while they were there.

They arrived at the hospital at 7:15 p.m. and inquired about Darla's room number. There was no record of Darla having been admitted, yet they knew that the Helms were to have checked her in early in the morning. After some confusion, the three women were told to go to the nursing office. There, staff in charge said that they were "being cautious." Apparently they were worried that the press might "make a case" out of the sterilization or some other aspect of Darla's situation. Clay staff were then sent to Darla's room, which was a private room at the end of the hall on the pediatrics—not the usual maternity—ward. It was fairly isolated from other patients' rooms. Carol, James, Dot, and Darla, all tense and upset, were present in the room. From the time the family arrived at 8 a.m. until 2 p.m., nothing had happened. Clay staff learned there was some mix-up and the anesthesiologist had not been given information; then he refused to do the tests because he had not been able to do them at the proper time. Later he agreed to do the required preoperative tests, but in the meantime there was a good deal of anxiety created among Southside Hospital staff and the Helms family.

Darla had dark circles around her eyes. She had not slept much the night before going to the hospital. She had been given thorazine at 5 p.m. and was groggy, but she still got up three or four times during the night. Family members had tried to direct her back to bed, but she was restless in bed, rolling around, and upset because she could not sleep on her stomach. Teresa Bellows gave this description of that night's mood:

> The night before surgery Darla was doped up and she was trying hard to stay awake. She knew that something was up. The parents resented the hospital staff for planning to keep Darla in restraints. They were vehement against restraints. They were bothered about the heavy dosage of medication that Darla was receiving. At one point Darla pinched Carol. Carol said, "No hurting." Dot was a basket case. As far as Dot is concerned Darla is "her baby." Dot dotes on Darla something ferocious. Dot had to be taken out when Darla got medical care. The family looked worn out, especially Carol. They looked happy to see us. James said several times that he was pleased that we were there. (I don't know if he was just saying that.)

At about 8:15 p.m. Darla vomited three times and there was no basin. James went to get a nurse. Jana Jones, an obstetrical nurse, finally came at about 8:40 p.m. She was calm and slow-moving and talked a lot to Carol and had a calming influence on the family group. By 8:45 p.m. Darla was sound asleep. Jones and Carol felt for contractions for about 20 to 25 minutes, but they could not feel any. They all watched the university basketball game on television and Carol and Dot went out for a smoke. They listened to the baby's heartbeat, which Jones declared to be a strong one. Then the Clay staff went to a nearby motel to spend the night.

Jana Jones was the obstetrical nurse who cared for Darla personally and who would direct the other nurses who cared for Darla during her 5 days in the hospital. Although she usually worked on the maternity ward, she had been assigned to Darla on the pediatrics floor. She came down from obstetrics to do checks on Darla and was always available on call. Jones would be responsible for getting Darla to the operating room. Jones had been a nurse for 9 years, yet she was very nervous and unsure as she anticipated Darla's arrival at the hospital. She and the other nurses had been involved in the inservice session about Darla conducted by the hospital social worker and Clay Center personnel. Although a confident and gregarious young woman, Jones admitted to having been very frightened at the prospect of caring for the girl she had seen on the videotape. During their first few hours together, Jones found herself panicking at every movement Darla made. Nursing school had never really prepared her for such an experience, and she felt little confidence as she anticipated nursing an autistic patient through birth. Jones had experience with patients with disabilities on the maternity ward and in caring for girls even younger than Darla who were having babies, but Darla was unique because of her total inability to communicate. Jones was used to explaining everything she was doing to her patients and to listening to their concerns. She followed the same procedures with Darla but was frustrated by the recognition that Darla was not comprehending anything that was said. Jones confessed to Clay staff when family were out of the room, "I'm new at this. I feel helpless and inadequate." But Clay staff judged her to be very good at her job, "caring and gentle," and Darla responded well to her. Jones was particularly encouraging and supportive with Carol.

The Day of the Surgery

For the day of the surgery, Dr. Franklin had extra operating room help because he suspected there might be medical problems with the baby. Furthermore, he had the additional responsibility of drawing blood from Darla, from the baby's umbilical cord, and from the three male members of Darla's family who were possible suspects of paternity. Paul Bettendorf, the Hudson County prosecuting attorney, had ordered the blood tests at the request of the county juvenile judge and had also required that Donna Karnes, the Hudson County child protection worker, be present during the birth and blood tests. Karnes had never been in an operating room or witnessed the birth of a baby, other than her own, so Dr. Franklin had the additional worry about the possibility of an adverse reaction on her part. Although he had more staff in the operating room than he would have had in normal circumstances, in retrospect Franklin felt that he should have had even more help present during that time.

When the Clay staff returned to the hospital at 7:35 a.m., they found Dot, James, Carol, and Sharon (a girl in her early twenties who had apparently lived with the Helms as a teenager, because of some family difficulty) waiting. James was in a surgical gown. After Carol failed to convince Darla to sit in the wheelchair that was to take her to the operating room, James eventually succeeded. There, at 7:15, Darla had been given a shot, and had an I.V., a catheter, and a tube through her nose to her stomach inserted. James had stayed with Darla until she was "out" and then returned to join his relatives in the waiting room. Karnes went into the operating room after James came out. James was quiet, but was described as "good support" for the women. Carol was "in charge." Dot was emotional. Pieces of conversation were floating around; James said, "This is a waiting game." When the conversation turned to the baby's gender, James joked, "You girls sound like you have your bookies." Dot talked about Darla when she was a little girl as their "light and joy." Apparently Darla used to say "no ciggies" when her grandmother and mother smoked. At one point Dot said, "I'd like to know who did this to her." Everyone was tired, especially Carol.

At 7:45 Jana Jones came out, hugged Carol, and said that Darla was "fine." She said the baby was a boy. Probably because Darla was heavily sedated prior to the Caesarean section, her son, Jason, had trouble breathing immediately after he was born and had to be resuscitated. He did not cry and the nurse conjectured that the baby was sleepy from Darla's medication. At 8:10 a.m. the baby was wheeled out of the operating room and taken to the Neonatal Intensive Care Unit for monitoring. The family and Clay staff were invited to see him. He had a tube through his nose to help with his breathing. Clay staff agreed that his color was good and he was a good size, though quiet. After the baby was taken away, they all went back to the waiting room. James remarked, "That's the little rascal that caused all the trouble." Carol claimed, "He's blond. That's no Helm!" to her mom and husband. Dot asked Carol, "Feeling good grandma?" Carol said, "I don't care about him; I want to see Darla."

At 8:20 a.m. James's mother, his brother Dale, and Darla's brother Jimmy arrived. There were hugs and announcements all around. Shortly after, Donna Karnes came out to the waiting room. She had watched the birth, although she said that she had hardly seen the baby. In the middle of the surgery she felt weak and had to sit down. Dr. Franklin came out and announced that Darla was doing well, but he talked to the family about his concern about their caring for the baby in their home. He said he was worried about what Darla might do to the baby. Dot announced that they knew all that, that they'd had to watch Darla when Missy was born. At 8:55 a.m., James went to the recovery room. Hospital staff wanted him there when they put Darla in restraints. Dale and Jimmy went with Donna Karnes to the lab for their blood tests related to the paternity investigation. James returned and reported that Darla was waking up. Then he followed the other men for his blood test.

At this point seven family members, three Clay Center staff, Donna Karnes, and Thomas Franklin were present in the waiting room. Teresa Bellows recalled:

> It was really a circus that morning. Remarks were flying everywhere. I was trying to absorb as much as possible of what went on. I was trying to keep out of the way and yet be helpful. The family was embarrassed because of the blood tests, but otherwise they seemed to be comfortable with Clay staff and they acted like they were happy we were there.

The three Clay staff members went to the nursery for about 45 minutes. Darla's baby looked big, healthy, and pink compared with the others in the Neonatal Intensive Care Unit. By 9:30 a.m. Darla was back in her room with everybody there. Meanwhile Donna Karnes returned saying that she needed pictures of the men. There was a search through wallets for pictures. Dot had some group pictures that included Jimmy and Darla, but she refused to part with them. They were her favorite pictures. Everyone laughed at Dot about that. Carol stated, "If they had any sense they wouldn't do these tests." Darla was sleeping and so the family went out for breakfast.

Jana Jones came in to care for Darla. Throughout the day a parent or Clay staff assisted as Jones massaged Darla's uterus and pushed out blood. She did this once an hour for 6 hours, then the night shift did it once every 2 hours six more times. Darla was sedated and calm following surgery and throughout these procedures. Jones was frequently in the room with Darla.

Later in the day, Dot was in the room with Darla and Clay staff while the others went to see the baby. Although Clay staff had agreed not to ask questions, Dot volunteered considerable information and seemed herself to be genuinely concerned about the paternity of the baby. Several times they heard her ask aloud, "Who did this to Darla?" At one point she said that Freddy, an elderly neighbor, might be a possibility. Carol had seemed relieved that the baby's hair wasn't dark like her husband's and son's, which she implied ruled out the men in her family as responsible for the pregnancy. When Carol was not there, Dot noted that Grandmother Helm's hair was red and James's sister was blond. She also speculated that it might be young kids, Jimmy's friends. She confided that Darla never went beyond the swings in the yard. She reminisced about Darla's childhood, remembering that Darla had talked as a baby, saying "baba," "grandpa," and "dog." Dot told the staff members that when Jimmy and Darla were young she was unable to take care of the two of them by herself. She said Darla ran into walls. She speculated that Carol and James would keep the baby, saying Carol had a baby bed ready for him at home. Although Dot felt James did not want a boy, he wanted a girl, she said, "He'll keep him, he'll want him!" She then remembered, "Last night he said 'Don't be upset if we don't keep him.'" Dot definitely wanted the family to keep the baby.

During the afternoon Clay staff members stayed with Darla so the family could have a break. When they left at 8 p.m. to make the 3-hour trip home, Darla's family thanked them profusely. All three Clay Center staff felt good about the support their presence had given Darla and her family, but when they stopped to have supper before the long drive home, they realized how totally exhausted they were.

The Hospital Stay

Bill Peterson and Kelly Fincher, another staff member, went to the hospital the following day. Carol, James, and Dot had been there all day and all night for more than 2 days and were "pretty shot." They were pleased to be able to leave the hospital and take some breaks. Again, Dot chatted with Clay staff, telling them about Darla's early days. She said that Darla was the "apple of her eye," her "first grandchild." She was openly angry at whoever had made Darla pregnant and confided that Darla "did not like people around her," so she was surprised this had happened. James said that he was anxious to have Darla back at the Clay Center.

When Darla woke up and saw her Clay Center friends, she was very affectionate. Fincher said she was surprised at how affectionate Darla could be. When she was out of bed, Darla wanted to sit on people's laps. She was still heavily sedated but when she woke up she was restless. She wanted to get up and she seemed not to be able to get comfortable anyplace. According to Peterson: "We signed bathroom and she indicated that she wanted to go. We eventually asked for pain medicine for her because she was getting unruly."

On the third day, Brad Parley and Margie Jasper took their turn at Mapleton Hospital. Darla looked pale to them and was unsteady on her feet, but Parley noted: "She was a model patient—unusually calm and pleasant. I think because of the medication she did not create problems. She slept a lot." With her usual concern about medicine, Carol was resistant to Franklin's suggestions that sedatives be used when she returned to Clay Center. Jasper agreed, saying, "It was my opinion that the level of sedation she was on would have interfered with her learning. In most cases I'm opposed to medication." Parley was impressed with the family, whom he had not met before that day. He observed: "It was obvious that the mom and grandma really loved Darla and took good care of her. Darla had strong bonds with them. They were tired, but they were still on top of her needs. They had projects for her to do."

By Friday, when Pam Brookshire and Felicia Tudor arrived at the hospital, Darla's condition was considerably improved. James had been back at work for the past 2 days, and Carol and Dot were in a good mood. They took full advantage of Clay staff presence and left for a long period of time. They did some shopping in preparation for taking Darla and Jason home. Tudor described Darla's last day in the hospital.

> Upon our arrival Darla was in bed. She took our hands, smiled and hugged us. Then she got up, grabbed our hands and led us on a "tour" of the hospital, showing us the halls, bathrooms, and the playroom.

She stopped to straighten the toys in the playroom. Back in the room she got into the arts and crafts suitcase that we had brought for her to use at home during her recuperation period before she returned to the Clay Center. She was smiling and happy. She glued a collage and wove a new reed/ribbon placemat. She sat on my lap and indicated that she wanted to look through a shopping bag that I had with me. She laughed and giggled when I gave her Eskimo kisses. While she was awake she was alert and active and did not seem to be in much pain. After she got a pain pill she slept for a couple of hours. We woke her up when her lunch tray arrived. She got up to sit in a chair to eat. She ate independently, even opening the sealed containers by herself.

All of those who went to the hospital felt that Darla's behavior was significantly better than they had anticipated. She seemed pleased with her room and the attention she was getting, and she interacted fairly well with the hospital staff. She left her dressings and stitches alone. According to Carol:

> Darla did very well in the hospital. She was better than she has ever been. I don't know why. It was strange behavior for Darla. You couldn't get her to do it again. Sometimes I don't know what goes through her head. I had described Darla to the hospital staff ahead of time and they expected a monster. What they got was an angel. They must have thought I was pretty weird. Clay staff were surprised how good she was.

Clay staff were glad they had gone to the hospital. They felt their presence was a help to both family and hospital staff. This perception was confirmed by the comments of Carol, James, Dr. Franklin, and various Mapleton Hospital employees.

News of Jason's Condition

Jason was 19 inches long and weighed 6 pounds 12 ounces. The first negative news—that he was having breathing problems—had been anticipated because of Darla's medication prior to his birth, and was considered temporary, not life-threatening. The family and friends present at the hospital were allowed to see Jason on his way to the Neonatal Intensive Care Unit. They described him as cute, good-sized, and having a healthy complexion.

It was not long after Jason's birth that Dr. Franklin sought out Carol to inform her that the baby's head was too small, and that a neonatal doctor had been called in for a second opinion. Franklin told Carol that this condition was called microcephaly and was associated with some degree of mental retardation, but the extent could not be determined at that point. Upset at this news, Carol's immediate response was to deny it, saying that Franklin did not want them to keep the baby and was trying to "make up problems" to get them to give the child up. She also felt that he was "just looking for problems" because of Darla's condition. Carol was very defensive about Darla's ability to bear a normal child. After her conference with Franklin, Carol came crying to the Neonatal Intensive Care Unit to look at the baby. Carol was on the point of collapse. Franklin was the focus of a lot of her anger, since Carol felt that he had handled giving her the news about Jason's condition poorly and coldly.

Dot's first response was to worry about the effect of the news on Carol, who had already been through so much, but she was also worried because, as she said: "They'll never take the baby home now. James won't let her. He won't let her go through it all again like she did with Darla." Dot was skeptical about the doctors' motives and suspicious about the accuracy of the diagnosis: "I know, because Darla is autistic, they were looking for things to be wrong with the baby." She turned to Clay Center staff and said, "Now tell me what you think of the baby. He looks fine to me!" James, too, challenged the diagnosis, saying: "I know the baby is all right. They're throwing a wrench in this to mix us up. They should let the Clay Center staff assess it. They're the experts." He proceeded to ask the nurses if Clay staff could examine the infant. Turning to the three, he said: "I want you ladies' opinion. You'd like to see him, wouldn't you? Do you see his head? Do you see anything the matter with it?" He then turned to McCormick, who was pregnant, and said, "We'll send Darla back to the Clay Center and you can cure her fast; then she can sit with you when you have your baby."

On Thursday, 4 days after the delivery, the family was still reluctant to accept the doctors' opinion that Jason was microcephalic. Carol announced that some test results had come back the day before that "proved" that Jason was normal. When Franklin arrived, she confronted him: "Would you be telling me that the baby has a small head if Darla weren't his mother?" Franklin kindly and patiently explained that the tests given Jason to determine whether there was premature skull fusion indicated that this did not appear to be the case—that the X-rays were indeed "normal," but that this did not mean that Jason was not microcephalic. He reaffirmed the fact that the head measurements were smaller than normal—that Jason was microcephalic. Carol simply was not willing to believe his diagnosis. After he left, Carol announced: "Doctors don't know about autism. Darla may not be brain-damaged and Jason might not be either." Franklin told Clay staff that he had recommended that chromosome tests be done on Jason, but the Helms refused, saying they saw no reason to do them.

The rules for an infant leaving the Neonatal Intensive Care Unit were

that it must weigh at least 5 pounds, be able to eat food by mouth, breathe on
its own, and maintain body temperature. Jason's weight was fine and his vital
signs were stabilizing as well. Other than the microcephalic condition, Jason
appeared to be a healthy baby.

Decisions About Child Rearing

At the hospital, the day after Jason's birth, the focus of attention was on the
future of Darla's baby. Carol doggedly talked about her concern about what
to do about Jason. Eventually Carol and James went off by themselves to
discuss the situation. When they returned, they announced that they had
decided to keep the baby. He was Darla's baby, their grandchild, and they
were going to care for him in their family. They knew they could love him.
They seemed relieved to have made the decision. Dot was ecstatic.

MEDICAL CARE FOR JASON

After microcephaly had been diagnosed, Dr. Franklin and Clay personnel
recommended that the Helms take Jason to see Dr. Shelley Hunt in Capital
City. Hunt, a pediatrician, medical geneticist, and Director of the Newborn
Follow-Up Program at Children's Hospital, sees infants who are diagnosed
at birth as having disabilities. Subsequently, Dr. Edge and two other pediatricians referred the Helms to Dr. Hunt. Nevertheless, it took them 4 months
to make the initial contact.

In the meantime, the Helms had taken Jason to Dr. Shelby in Mapleton,
who was the attending pediatrician at Jason's birth. Shelby asked the family
to sign papers relinquishing parental rights so that Jason could be institutionalized or placed for adoption, because he felt that Jason was a "profoundly
retarded child" who should not be reared in their home. The Helms were
upset at this and switched doctors. Edge refused to provide medical care for
Jason because he thought that a child with disabilities should be seen by a
pediatrician rather than a general practitioner. The Helms refused to go to
Anthony Wilder because of conflicts they had had with him in the past over
Darla, so they traveled to a city about the same distance as Mapleton, but in
the opposite direction, for Jason's pediatric care. For reasons similar to her
rejection of previous doctors, Carol was no more pleased with the new pediatrician than she had been with the others. Moreover, as time passed, Carol
began to make her own observations about Jason. The growth of his body
made the smallness of his head obvious. Carol was sophisticated enough about
infant development to recognize that Jason was "slow." Carol also had
observed Jason to have what she thought were seizures, and the doctor con-

firmed the likelihood of Jason having a seizure disorder. By the time Jason was 4 months old, Carol was ready to make an appointment with a doctor who specialized in the care of infants with handicapping conditions.

Dr. Hunt's examination of Jason confirmed previous medical diagnoses: Jason is a "true microcephalic baby with a very underdeveloped brain." Although the extent of retardation could not be determined at that time, Hunt told the Helms that Jason would very likely be severely retarded. Hunt reported that Jason was clean and appeared to be well-cared for. She remarked that Carol obviously loved the baby and was an attentive and concerned caretaker.

While at Children's Hospital, Jason was examined by an ophthalmologist who said that the constant roving and jerking motion of Jason's eyes as he tried to focus on objects was a condition called *nystagmus*, which due to an underdeveloped optic nerve, results in decreased visual acuity.

Hunt said that the Helms first discussed Jason's diagnosis and prognosis in a rational manner, although they kept pushing for absolute answers about his future. They wanted to know how retarded Jason would be and whether he would learn to talk. They inquired whether his condition was associated with behavior problems, as is autism. Carol also asked if Jason could have surgery to open up the skull and perhaps provide a plate as a substitute covering for the brain so that "Jason's brain could grow" and retardation could be prevented. (X-rays taken after his birth had disclosed that his skull bones were not fused, and, in fact, microcephaly results from an underdeveloped brain that does not grow and not from a skull that blocks brain growth.)

Hunt recalled that Carol inquired about institutional alternatives, stating that Darla had made her fully aware of the impact that a child with disabilities could have on a family. Carol conveyed that they had put a great deal of serious thought into the decision to keep Jason and confessed that they still wavered and had doubts about the wisdom of their decision. She indicated that they would not be opposed to institutional care if Jason grew up to be as difficult to raise as Darla. Hunt tried to provide information that was realistic but not unduly negative. She also tried to be a good listener as the Helms reflected on the future.

The Helms remained "calm and rational" until they asked—and were told—about the probable cause of Jason's condition. Hunt's response was that it was her belief that Jason's pathological conditions resulted from incest. She explained to the Helms that microcephaly was a recessive gene disorder, and recessive gene disorders are likely to occur in cases of incest because a parent and child, or brother and sister, have half their genes in common. If the microcephalic gene was present in the Helm family, Darla's chances, in the case of incest, of having a microcephalic child were one in four. Hunt told the Helms that Jason's microcephalic condition was probably not related to his mother's autism. Hunt discussed the chromosome studies of people with autism, which she said indicated the presence of "fragile X" in some cases. There was no evidence of a fragile X problem in Jason's blood studies.

When Hunt provided evidence of the etiology of Jason's microcephaly to the Helms, James was so belligerently skeptical about the information that she decided to take him to see a male geneticist colleague, Art Kincady. Dr. Kincady spent about "3 hours" with James and Carol, while the rest of the family sat in the corridor. Hunt observed the four children while they waited for their parents. Fourteen-year-old Jimmy was in charge of Darla, Missy, and Jason. Although Darla occasionally screamed and banged her head on the wall, Jimmy was fairly efficient in amusing and controlling his sisters as well as 5-month-old Jason.

Hunt was annoyed that the Helms cancelled several visits at the last minute, so she was unable to provide medical care for Jason for a number of months. Unaware that the Helms were taking Jason to another pediatrician, Hunt felt that more frequent follow-up care was needed for a baby like Jason.

WORRIES ABOUT JASON

Concern about people with mental retardation bearing children dates back to over a century ago when social Darwinism and eugenic theories first took hold of the public's imagination (Stepan, 1991; Thurman, 1985). Although the eugenic position was heavily criticized and the movement underwent a severe decline in response to the genocides associated with World War II (Stepan, 1991), traces of eugenics thinking are still apparent in attitudes toward people with disabilities (Yuker, 1988). Most participants in this study admitted to not being particularly surprised to hear that Darla's baby had a disability; however, they wavered between attributing his conditions to genetic causes and to environmental causes.

Medical professionals' first concern was about the congenital abnormalities that result from incest, but they also were worried about the effects of the prenatal environment. Andrew Edge's response was fairly typical.

> First, she was sexually abused, well . . . used . . . , and if that was
> incest, then there are problems. Then, there was little control over
> her well-being during pregnancy; there could be no patient education
> and it was hard to control what Darla ate that might hurt the baby. I
> worried about her falling or hitting herself. I was also concerned
> about medication and treatment. I had given her some medicine for
> upset stomach when I didn't know she was pregnant during the first
> month of her pregnancy. She was physically fit, though. I was con-

cerned about the baby, but I had no real hunch about what it would
be like. Genetically there was no information available about reproduction in autistic females.

Clay staff worried that Darla's behavior created a less than optimal prenatal environment. As Brookshire said:

> I figured the baby would be high-risk for being handicapped. Darla
> was under stress because of moving to the Clay Center, she was self-
> abusive, she screamed a lot, she frequently hit her own stomach, she
> flopped down on her stomach.

Tokar explained:

> Darla would take a running dive toward her bed and would flop down
> on her stomach. She laid on her stomach up to the eighth month. I
> figured the baby would be retarded because of her constant scream-
> ing and headbanging. I thought it would be a miracle if the baby was
> born normal.

Some worried about prematurity and low birth weight because of Darla's age.
    Along with the fears went the hope that the baby would be normal. Yoder
said, "It would be nice if it could be normal; nice if Carol had something that
belonged to Darla, to always have part of her." A similar sentiment was
expressed by Ingalls.

> From a physical standpoint Darla is healthy—a healthier teenager
> than in many other teenage pregnancies. She should be more able to
> tolerate pregnancy than many girls her age. I saw Jason at the Clay
> Center at a case review. He was a fantastic little kid. When I think
> about Darla and how her mom had held out great hopes for her and
> how Darla has not been able to meet her mother's expectations, I
> thought, "Now Darla can give something tangible back to Mrs. Helm."
> She put a healthy infant back into the family. It was her way of giving
> something back to them like a nonautistic, normal girl could give back
> to her family.

Ingalls had already been told, on at least two occasions, that Jason was microcephalic and would probably be mentally retarded. Nevertheless, Ingalls told
both Fred Quail and Elise Yoder that the baby was normal. Optimistic, even
while recognizing the dangers, Jana Jones said, "I felt the possibility of problems with the child was great, but I have seen normal babies come from sick

women and bizarre situations." A common sentiment was that expressed by Lisa McNeil: "I know it sounds cruel, yet, if there are going to be retarded babies born, this one should be. It wouldn't have to face the personal situation."

Professional Concern About Jason

Many of those interviewed about the case confessed that prior to Jason's birth they had not thought much about his future; their concern was for Darla. After he was born, they tended to refer to Jason as "it," "the baby," or "Darla's baby," instead of "Jason" or "him," although many had seen Jason and could tell his sex and name when asked. In other words, they tended to deny his existence and depersonalize him. When questioned further, they voiced a wide variety of confused and ambivalent opinions about Jason's future.

Bill Peterson was one of a few who claimed to have had no hunches about the probable characteristics of Darla's baby prior to Jason's birth. During the interview, whenever he was questioned about the baby, he would change the subject. Confronted with his evasive behavior, he confessed that he "never" thought about the baby in connection with Darla's pregnancy and really did not want to think about Jason as an individual. It almost seemed that he had elected to blame Jason for Darla's problems and situation. This young man painfully admitted:

> I was apprehensive about being involved with the baby. I was really hit that something like this should happen. It was hard to get used to them being excited about the baby. I refused to see the baby. I finally looked in the infant care unit. I kept feeling, "This shouldn't be happening." I was shocked that the parents decided to keep the baby. I felt the infant would be better off in another situation. Another handicapped child is the last thing they need. The family has been through so much with Darla. It's unreal to expect them to care for another handicapped child, even though they'd deal OK. I just thought, "Couldn't someone else raise this one?" Their dealings with Darla aren't over. I don't see how they can take one crisis after another. If Carol is going to do this she ought to go into it professionally. If they didn't have the baby around, there'd be a hell of a lot less to explain. Explaining how Darla is the mother of a baby will isolate the family even more than they already are. I didn't accept the fact that a baby would result from the pregnancy. I couldn't face it.

Lisa McNeil said: "They're not well-off financially. I don't know if they can afford to bring up a baby. I'm not sure it's the best environment for the baby. I think they should put it up for adoption." Jerry Roderick said: "I question whether the family can handle another child with problems. I hate to see the child not get the care it needs right away. If Darla could have had constructive training early she would be better off now." Cindy McCormick simply responded, "I think they should have given it up for adoption." Teresa Bellows said:

> At first we thought the baby should definitely be taken away from them. It's sad. I'm kind of confused. I'm not sure it's microcephalic. I thought maybe the doctors were manipulating just to get the Helms to give the baby up. I'm confused. I don't know how to feel about the baby. I have to admit the baby is going to be loved. It couldn't get more love elsewhere. James said, "There's the little stinker who caused all the problems." He seems to care about him. I'm torn.

A number of respondents said that they admired the Helms for keeping Jason, especially after they learned that he was retarded. They perceived the Helms as "good parents" and thought that they would provide a loving home for Jason. Some said they respected the Helms' sense of family responsibility in caring for a child that they had allowed to come into the world. A recreation assistant said, "They're brave taking the baby. It's a big step."

In Winthrop, Laidlaw observed: "They show him around like a normal grandchild. They're upset with a doctor who suggested institutionalization—they changed pediatricians." Edge said:

> The baby is supposed to be doing well. They wanted to bring him here, but I felt that, since he's microcephalic, they should see a pediatrician. The Helms describe a real good baby. They called here to ask if microcephaly could be determined at birth. They didn't want to believe Dr. Franklin's diagnosis. They've accepted the baby. They carry him around. I'm not worried about the baby's care. The family is nurturing, caring, supportive—regardless of the child.

The obstetrical nurse, Jana Jones, who interacted with the Helm family only while Darla was in the hospital, felt there might be other motivations behind the Helms keeping Jason: "All I can think is that abortion would have been best. The Helms maybe should not have been allowed to make the decision for Darla to go ahead and have the baby. They had to keep that baby once it was born. They were worried that people would have looked at Carol as if she was hardened. It's difficult to give a baby up."

Parenting Jason

Although others anticipated difficulties, the Helms had been optimistic and were shocked and grieved by the baby's condition. Even several months after his birth, when his developmental delays were obvious to others, Carol peri-odically denied the diagnosis of microcephaly.

Carol still has confused and ambivalent feelings about keeping Jason. She had not wanted another child and had a tubal ligation when Missy was born. Before Jason's birth, Carol and James had vacillated between keeping the baby and placing it for adoption, and had decided to be "selfish" and not keep the baby if he were autistic or retarded like his mother. They did not want to be "tied down" again with the responsibility of a disabled child. In the end, their strong sense of family won out. They kept Jason even though they learned on the day of his birth that he was microcephalic and likely to be severely retarded. Carol said they could have made the decision to give up the baby before it was born, but it was hard to do that afterward. She said, "It's easy to give away something you don't have. If we let him go, we would never see him again. We looked at Jason and he looked so helpless. We knew he had problems, but we wanted what was best for him. We thought about what we could live with. He was our grandson and we couldn't give away what was ours."

Almost a year later, James recalled: "We did not make the decision for 2 or 3 days. We watched him in the hospital and tried to ask questions and find out about him. We wanted the truth. We looked at the baby and knew that there was not much wrong with him." (It is interesting that James was able to make this statement after raising his severely retarded and disturbed, but normal-looking, daughter.) James claimed that he counseled Carol not to let "the experts" influence their decision, saying: "I didn't think that the credentials of the doctor allowed an 'expert opinion' on whether or not Jason would be mentally retarded. We had the sense all along that he did not want us to keep Darla's baby and that he thought, because she was autistic, her baby would be handicapped, too. So we really tried to ignore what Dr. Franklin was telling us."

Two days after Jason's birth, his grandparents decided to take him home and raise him as their son. It was not an easy decision to make, and both admit they wavered back and forth before and after Jason's birth. Yet, James was able to conclude:

> Really, there was no decision to make. He was my grandson. I had to take him home. I've had fun with Jason, but he is often a handful. He might turn out to have more problems than Darla. We can see a few problems. We're still watching. For a while his development seemed to stop, which got Carol tense and worried. It seems like his head might have stopped growing. But, lately, he has made progress. A lady from Mapleton came for a home visit and said he's at about 9 months (when he was 11 months old). She said that was good. Anyway, I made the decision to keep him and I can't say that I goofed up.

Although others felt that Carol talked James into agreeing to keep Jason, James insists that he really made the decision. James also denies that Dot influenced them, saying, "I was the one who could not give away my own flesh and blood."

James calls Jason "a fine little fellow," whom they are "enjoying." When asked if they would reconsider keeping Jason, James replies: "Carol has too many hours of sitting up all night invested in him. If anyone took him away now it would kill her." James did not say too much about his feelings except that he and Carol had been looking forward to their three children getting older so they could do some things on their own. "Now," he said, "We have postponed being free by a minimum of 6 years (Jason is 6 years younger than Missy), and if he is as retarded as everyone thinks he might be, our freedom may be postponed indefinitely."

Carol refers to Jason as "our son" and calls herself "Mom." She is delighted when his babbling includes "maaa" sounds. "He is a good-natured baby, almost too good," says Carol. When Jason was 7 months old, the interviewer observed him responding to his grandmother's hugs and kisses with smiles. Although he was large for his age and his head had grown more than doctors expected, Jason appeared developmentally delayed. He responded like a 2- to 3-month-old infant. Carol still hoped that he would not be retarded, but also seemed resigned to that probability.

If Jason turns out to be as severely handicapped as Darla and requires as much of their time and energy, Carol states that she is determined "not be so stupid and keep him for 16 years." She is a little vague about the "outside help" they will seek to care for him. She stresses that their knowledge of how a child with severe handicaps disrupts family life and consumes everyone's energy has made her "swear not to go through it again." She speculates that her will "to keep" will not be as strong with Jason as it was with Darla, because she knows the reality it entails. Carol said, "If he is a holy terror like Darla, we will not keep him. But if there's a sense that he knows us and living with us can make a difference, we'll keep him. At least I hope he's more verbally normal so that he can communicate with us. I also feel like when he progresses, he won't then lose ground, like happened with Darla."

Carol seems pleased with 7-month-old Jason's progress, which she estimates to be "right on the charts." She notes that her other children had been "ahead on the charts," so she assumes that even this is a bad sign. Carol recalls being told that, since Jason had no soft spots on his head, it would not grow at all. She notes that, contrary to expectations, his head has grown. Then unexpectedly, Carol laughs and admits that when she and Dot went shopping recently and saw other babies, they remarked to each other how "weird they look with their big heads." They were getting used to Jason.

As usual, there was friction with James's parents. Carol was disappointed by their response to Jason.

They treat Jason as if he has leprosy. They won't go near him. They
have only been to visit us twice since he was born 7 months ago, even
though they live just 2 minutes away. When they visit, they don't ask
to see him. They've told us to "put him away." They never offer to
take care of the children and yet they tell other people they take care
of our kids all the time. When I hear that I set whoever says it
straight. It annoys me that she [James's mother] pretends to act like a
grandmother to other people when she doesn't even acknowledge his
[Jason's] presence to us.

Darla's Response to Jason

People wondered whether Darla would show maternal instinct. In the end,
most agreed that Darla had no awareness of her pregnancy or of a "mothering" role in relation to the infant she delivered. Of course, it is unclear how
an autistic person with more cognitive awareness than Darla has would have
responded. Clay staff, who had helped at the hospital, shared their recollections of Darla's reactions to her baby. Felicia Tudor observed:

> At the hospital Darla was aware that something was up, but they had
> her medicated so she mainly slept. Dot, Carol, and Darla went down
> to "see the baby." Darla was there but she did not pay any attention to
> the baby. Dot and Carol pointed Jason out and said, "Look, Darla,
> there is your baby," but Darla did not react. She indicated that she
> wanted to go to the game room. She did not seem to see the connec-
> tion between her pregnancy and the baby. There was no realization
> that it was her baby.

Another said, "I saw her glimpse at the baby, but I don't think she realized it
was connected with her pregnancy. She is so far gone—she has no sense that
it's her baby." Some confessed to hoping that Darla would show nurturing
instinct and prove that maternal instinct was not affected by intelligence or
autism. One lamented: "Childbearing is a natural animal act, but somehow
she doesn't know she has a kid and she can't even go through a natural mothering process."

After visiting Darla during her maternity leave from Clay, Fincher noted:
"When I went to the Helms' trailer I never saw Darla deliberately go look at
the baby. But Carol told me that Darla did hold Jason and tried to kiss him
on the forehead. I don't think there was a real awareness of the baby. As far
as I could see she was more interested in his toys than in Jason. She picked
up his rattles and played with them." Brookshire said: "I watched Carol have

Darla hold Jason. Carol was the one interested in this procedure, not Darla. Darla has no idea—she can't differentiate between babies, animals, or dolls."

After Darla returned to the Clay Center, McNeil noticed: "Darla tears up her doll babies, thumps them around, or masturbates with them—she does not cuddle them." Parley said:

> She has no concept of the baby. Her family would love for her to feel maternal toward the baby. Carol has not accepted Darla's autism. They hoped the pregnancy might cure her. But Darla is not attuned to the baby. They brought Jason to the Clay Center when they were picking Darla up for a home visit. Paula (another client) grabbed the baby and said, "Hurt baby!" Paula is mesmerized by babies. She wants to make them cry. But Darla just ignored Jason.

A number of Clay staff hypothesized that one reason the Helms let Darla go through with the pregnancy was that they hoped an attachment to the baby might improve her condition. One staff member even quoted Carol as having made such a statement.

Jasper had anticipated that Darla would be jealous of the attention paid to Jason, but noted: "It was not Darla, but Carol, who was bonding with Jason. Darla did not seem jealous—she really did not even seem to notice." Tokar observed:

> You won't get a picture of the "loving mother" with Darla. She'll feel no responsibility toward it. She probably was not aware of the pregnancy; it's hard to know. She could perhaps put it together if she'd been around other births. But put her baby in a room full of babies and she wouldn't go pick it out. If it was crying she wouldn't go feed it. She can hardly take care of herself.

The family's lawyer, Carl Laidlaw, felt: "Darla doesn't have the emotional, intellectual, or verbal skills to have a relationship with her baby. She doesn't know what the concept of mother is, although she has a close relationship with her own mother."

Carol credits Darla with being aware that Jason came from her body, however, and maintains that when Darla comes home on visits she always heads for Jason's crib. Once Carol found Darla holding Jason rather precariously on her outstretched arms. She had gone to his crib to pick him up. Carol approached Darla calmly and cautiously; she knew if she screamed and ran at her, as she felt like doing to rescue the baby, Darla would probably drop Jason or throw him. Although Carol believes that Darla understands more than most people give her credit for, Carol knows that Darla is not capable of caring for Jason.

James also believes that Darla is aware that Jason is her baby. According to James, when Darla was home at Christmas, she kept restlessly looking around. She got fidgety, then she took off down the hallway and saw Jason in his crib. After that she calmed down and sat down and behaved. James says that Darla was never able to hold Missy when she was a baby, but has been able to hold Jason fairly gently.

CHAPTER 5

Paternity

The newborn, fortunately, was not aware of the uncertainty and suspicion surrounding his birth. Although his father was present in the hospital on the day of his birth, and was at the trailer when Jason was brought home from the hospital, he did not confess his part in the pregnancy until Jason was 6 months old and the evidence against him was undeniable. Shortly thereafter, Jason's father began to receive counseling at the Winthrop Mental Health Center.

CAROL'S WORRIES ABOUT PATERNITY

In an interview several months after Jason's birth, when Carol was asked about the paternity of the baby, she evasively said she did not know. She said Jimmy had been cleared twice by blood tests, and the results of the third blood test had not been received. Carol then reported the time that Darla had "run off" for a short time, implying that she could have been raped by a stranger. Yet Carol frequently had assured others that Darla had "never been out of her sight" during the summer months.

According to Carol, Darla's sexual drives and feelings were apparent in "rides on the arm of the couch" and masturbating with various objects. Once Carol saw Darla pushing a hard plastic giraffe at her genitals. Dot was there when this occurred. When Carol called her mother to tell her of Darla's pregnancy, Dot first asked, "Who did it? Who would have done such a thing?" and then said, "Maybe it was the giraffe." Carol laughed when she told this story, and she recalled, "I was crying away on the phone and my mom says that. She's a nut. She always sees the humor in things." A number of other relatives and friends shared their theories about Darla's pregnancy with Carol. One of James's brothers said he had heard of someone getting pregnant in the swimming pool. Carol's response was, "Don't be stupid!" Even though Carol had observed incidents indicating sexual drive, she felt that Darla would not "throw herself in someone's bed." If she happened to be there, chances are that she would not fight or complain, but she would not initiate sex. In Carol's opinion, "she doesn't ask for it."

During the same interview, a few hours after her denial of knowledge of the paternity of the baby, Carol suddenly confessed:

> I don't like to lie. I might as well tell the truth. Jimmy is the one who did it. [After a pause, Carol gave an account of her reactions.] When I first found out for sure, I wanted to strangle him. I hated him. How could he be so stupid? So cruel? So irresponsible? It tore his Daddy up. His Daddy still won't speak to him. He violated our trust. Here he is so respectable in this town—the model boy, the model student— and he goes and does this. He's got a good reputation here in Winthrop—at school and in the town. His relatives all think he's great. He's an "A" student, he's not into drugs or alcohol, he's polite and well-mannered, he behaves himself, he's quiet but popular with the kids and teachers, he doesn't get into fights, and everybody thinks he's so responsible. So respectable. Well, he had them fooled. He had us all fooled. We thought we could trust him.

When Carol first learned of the pregnancy, she was upset and angry at whoever had "raped Darla." Darla had been carefully supervised throughout the summer. She had been left only with James, Jimmy, and James's brother Dale and Dale's girlfriend. She remembered only one time that Darla had been unsupervised. Carol was washing her car when Darla disappeared. Carol found her about 20 minutes later sitting in a mud puddle down the road, and nobody else was in sight. Jimmy suggested that his friends had been around during the summer, but Carol did not remember any of them being alone with Darla.

Right from the start Carol realized that the perpetrator might be someone in her immediate family. Others were hinting that the father of Darla's baby was either her husband or her son. What is more, she knew that the Welfare Department and the Prosecuting Attorney had asked to have blood tests done on the three male family members who had access to Darla when she was alone. Carol had to live with the suspicion that the person who had sexual intercourse with Darla might be one of the men who were closest to her.

When Carol first saw Jason she was relieved that his coloring was not similar to that of her own children, seeing this as evidence that a family member was not responsible for Darla's pregnancy. She hoped that this would prove true in the blood tests as well. Prior to Jason's birth, Carol had announced on several occasions that if the guilty party was a family member, he would no longer be allowed into her house.

Jimmy had been their perfect son. He was everything that Darla was not. Since he was fortunate in his healthy and normal condition, the Helms expected perfection from him. He did not have Darla's excuses to err. They were "stunned and shocked" by this sexual behavior, "torn up" as a family. Although Darla's problems had brought the family closer together, Jimmy's "problem" was "tearing them apart." James was furious at his son and they had not spoken in weeks. Carol was angry at Jimmy, but also hurt that he had not told the truth when they first discovered Darla's pregnancy.

When the results of the first blood tests came back in May, the prosecuting attorney, Paul Bettendorf, accused Jimmy of fathering the baby. The tests had cleared James and his brother Dale, but Jason's and Jimmy's blood composition matched. According to Carol, Bettendorf accused Jimmy without proper evidence and without following the correct procedures, which, due to a ruling called "double jeopardy," meant that he was not allowed to file the same charge against the same person even if he obtained better evidence. Carol felt that Bettendorf was "eager" to prosecute, but his "hands were tied" by the double jeopardy ruling. Nevertheless, even without the threat of legal prosecution, Carol was determined to prove Jimmy's innocence. When Bettendorf first accused Jimmy of the paternity of Darla's baby, he indicated that in the case of juveniles, usually counseling was recommended rather than time in a correctional institution. Apparently, incest among siblings is not considered to be child abuse, even when one of the partners is severely disabled. Bettendorf and Karnes insisted that the family start treatment at the Winthrop Mental Health Clinic. When the Helms challenged the validity of the blood test results and accused Winthrop authorities of "framing" them, the mandate for counseling was postponed.

The court ordered a second test for Jimmy and Jason. The results were again positive, but Jimmy still denied his guilt. James suspected his son after the second blood tests were positive, and even before. He pleaded with Carol to acknowledge the fact that Jimmy was guilty. Carol refused on the grounds that her son was honest and would not lie to her. Moreover, she had observed Jimmy's consistently kind and caring manner toward Darla and could not believe that he "raped her." Carol knew that the blood tests were supposed to be valid, but she had heard they might not be accurate when the baby's father was also a close relative of the mother. Because her son denied that he had touched Darla, Carol believed him and "fought for him."

They decided to get a blood test done on their own to clear their son. In August, a short time after their initial visit to Dr. Hunt, Carol called to ask her about the possibility of having blood tests done on her son and grandson for the purpose of proving that Jimmy had not fathered Darla's child. She explained that local authorities were trying to "pin the whole thing" on Jimmy and that they had "falsified evidence to frame her son." Her proof that the results were falsified was that Winthrop officials would not show the family the original laboratory report. Dr. Hunt said that Carol was very upset as they talked on the phone and Hunt worried that Carol might be having a "breakdown." Carol had previously informed Hunt about Darla's autistic condition, but she had also told her that Darla had become pregnant at the Clay Center and that the paternity of the baby was unknown. Hunt had already learned about the possibility of incest from personnel at the Clay Center shortly after Jason's first visit. After getting permission from Carol to obtain the lab reports, Hunt wrote to Bettendorf and asked for the blood test results. He did not respond to her inquiry and never sent the requested information.

Dr. Hunt attempted to convince Carol to accept the validity of the previous tests. The tests were expensive: $350 for the set of three tests for Darla, Jimmy, and Jason. Carol was determined to have the tests repeated and arranged to have a third set of blood samples drawn at Children's Hospital. It was far enough away that no one in Winthrop would know.

In early October, the results of the third blood tests arrived at the Helms' trailer by registered mail while Jimmy was in school. The Children's Hospital blood test results were the same as those done in Mapleton and in Winthrop. They established a 302 to 1 likelihood that Jimmy was Jason's father. Even the objective medical staff at the clinic assured Carol that the blood tests were indeed valid even in the case of incest.

Carol spent the day in turmoil. It was hard to continue to believe Jimmy, especially when she could not deny that somebody had made Darla pregnant, and Jimmy had been left alone with Darla on many occasions. When Jimmy returned from school, Carol told him about the blood test results and said that she would continue to believe his denial of guilt, but that his father did not. She also informed Jimmy that the unresolved situation was causing so much friction between James and herself that she was worried that their marriage would break up. Carol did not tell Jimmy that just to get a confession from him. In fact, for the first time in their marriage there was significant disagreement. She told Jimmy that if he was guilty she wanted the truth. Jimmy went to his room. He returned in about 30 minutes and confessed that he had engaged in sexual intercourse once with his sister.

After Jimmy's confession, the Helm family started therapy. Jimmy, Carol, and James were seen by a psychiatric social worker together and separately. The counselor was worried about Jimmy's depression and warned his parents that he might be suicidal. She cautioned the Helms to watch him closely.

Carol did not think that Jimmy had "raped" Darla because he was angry at his parents or resented his sister. She felt her son had "no cause" for such feelings. Although Carol admitted that Jimmy had taken on responsibilities for his sister beyond his years, it had been his "duty" because he was normal and she was not. Carol felt her son had, through the years, understood his responsibility and the reasons why it was necessary. She insisted that he had received the amount of attention "he deserved" from his family. Carol's version was that Jimmy was "foolishly experimenting" with sex with Darla. Jimmy said he had intercourse with Darla on only one occasion, but Carol suspected that this was not true. Carol did believe Jimmy's assertion that Darla was the only one he had had sex with—he had not had the opportunity to be alone with girls; they did not let him "run the streets."

Carol was incensed that there were places in town where teenagers could walk in and get condoms. She felt that making birth control so accessible encouraged teenagers to have sex; that it was "inviting innocents to experiment with sex." She knew of many high school girls who were pregnant or had children. Carol believed that bragging about one's sexual experience was a "bad thing" done by teenagers in town, but she had perceived her "responsible" Jimmy as being too smart for that. She thought he was "straight and narrow," but also informed—not a "dumb ass"— about sex. Carol concluded, "He should have known better."

Although most of Carol's feelings toward her son were hostile and angry, she occasionally showed some empathy: "I suppose all of Darla's open masturbation and her taking off her clothes and running through the house all the time was not easy for Jimmy. I know his hormones are active and he has sexual feeling. I guess that was arousing for him." But mostly Carol resented his having "taken advantage" of his sister. Carol was sure that, in spite of Darla's obvious sexual feeling and drive, Darla had not initiated sex with her brother, although she had been observed to initiate "arm wrestling." Even if Darla had approached her brother, it was still Jimmy's role to reject her. He was the one who knew better. Carol loved her son but it would be a "long time" before she would "trust him again." Carol's feelings toward Jimmy were ambivalent. She was furious at him for what he had done, but she also pitied his situation.

Carol emphasized that Jimmy's present suffering would not be short-lived. The result of his "selfishness and foolishness" was Jason. According to Carol, when Darla went away to the Clay Center, the rest of the family finally "had a chance" to be a "normal family," a "real family." Jimmy had "ruined it" for all of them by making Darla pregnant. Now they had another child with disabilities there to "interfere with a normal life." Jimmy had "destroyed things" for himself and his family. Carol said, "We had just a couple months of fun. Now we're back to the way we were. He may feel sorry for himself, but he is making our life hell. He's doing a damn good job of ruining our lives."

Carol knew that since the pregnancy had been discovered, people had been saying things like, "What kind of man would rape a girl like her?" or "I'd like to catch the son-of-a-bitch who did this to her." Jimmy had heard all these comments as he silently stood by. That was another way he "was paying" for his transgressions. Even now, people who did not know the truth of the situation made such comments in front of the family.

Jimmy's sterling reputation had now changed among people who knew of his guilt. James's parents had not yet been told that Jimmy was the father of Darla's baby. In the first place, Carol knew that it was just one more thing for which she would be blamed. Second, she felt that they would "spread it all over town." Carol wanted to spare Jimmy, and the rest of the family, that humiliation. She commented, "Jimmy does not deserve that. He's already hurting. Really hurting." Since the Helm family had kept to themselves for most of the time they lived in Winthrop, Carol felt that the present family situation was not generally known. She felt that acquaintances assumed that Jason was her son and, when she met people, that is what she told them.

Carol was reluctant to bring Darla home for a visit because she was afraid that "Jimmy would do it again." She commented, "What's to stop him now that Darla cannot have more children." However, Donna Karnes and Nancy, the Mental Health Counselor, told Carol that they thought that Jimmy would not attempt intercourse with Darla again. Both of them worried that Jimmy had negative feelings about Jason and were concerned about Jason's welfare. Carol was annoyed that Donna and Nancy "were not concerned about Darla—do not care what happens to her."

In January, 3 months after Jimmy's confession, things had somewhat calmed down in the Helm household, but, as Carol said, "We still have explosions around here. Mostly James has a hard time dealing with it. He's bruised real bad! He has a tendency to explode, then gets it off his chest and things get better for a while." Carol says, "In a way there's nothing normal around here. It will never be the way it was. We trusted Jimmy and it will be a long time before we trust again." Carol said that her own anger at Jimmy comes and goes. She still does not understand "quite what happened" and what motivated Jimmy "to do such a thing." As she said, "I fought for him and never would have believed the test—that's how much I trusted my son."

Like his parents, Jimmy still had "mood swings" and often seemed to be depressed. Jimmy was seeing Nancy, the counselor at the Mental Health Center, once a week. His parents usually accompanied him. According to James: "Jimmy likes Nancy. Nancy is easy to talk to and makes Jimmy talk. If he evades the truth she makes him face it. She won't take any flack from Jimmy. Jimmy would rather pretend that the whole thing did not happen, but Nancy will not let him forget or avoid problems."

Carol sounded as if she were talking about someone else's son when she cynically characterized Jimmy as "trying to play the role of the loving brother. When Jimmy comes home from school he helps with Jason, changing diapers, feeding him, and keeping him entertained. He is also very good to Missy, and when Darla is home he interacts with her as if nothing happened." Carol judged this behavior as "strange," "forced," "making himself go through the efforts to atone for his transgressions," but his actions might be covering his "real resentment toward Jason and Darla."

Carol had not softened her stand of blaming Jimmy as the sole guilty party. She insisted: "Darla can do no wrong. She has no understanding of right or wrong. Her masturbation and stripping did not help Jimmy, but they are no excuse. Jimmy knew better and he is to blame. Somehow he thought he could get away with it—thought he would not get caught—but Jason is the living proof that he couldn't."

Carol initially decided that she would be "Mom" to Jason, but then had second thoughts. She was confused and undecided about how she would handle their relationship. She wanted Jason to know that Darla was his mother; hence she wondered if he should not call her "Grandma" right from the start. On the other hand, she knew that Jason needed to call somebody "Mom," and Darla might not be around in his future. Carol felt that it would be good for Jason to know the truth about her being his grandmother right from the beginning, but thought it might be easier to have him call her "Mom" for a while. Although Carol had lingering doubts about the wisdom of their raising Jason, she was not angry at him. As she said, "Jason is innocent in all this. You can't blame anything on him. It's not his fault what happened. Even though we now know who the father is, we are keeping him. That's the bottom line."

Carol said that sometime she will tell Jason who his mother is; that he has the right to know. She states that one of Jason's parents has to be denied and "there is no denying Darla." She worries that he will hear in a negative fashion from someone else, so she hopes to be the first to tell him. But she wants to wait until he is "ready to know." She suggests that he may be 18 before he knows about the circumstances surrounding his birth. At one point, she confides that it might be best if he was retarded, because then he would not have to be aware of his situation or might not be so influenced by it. She feels that knowing about his parentage would be hard on him if he were of normal intelligence. On the other hand, if Jason were normal he might grow up with a sense of responsibility for taking care of his mother; then, as Carol says, "Some good will have come out of this mess."

Carol does not intend to tell Jason about his paternity, believing that it would only hurt him. In Carol's opinion, "being illegitimate is alright because it's fairly common, but this [incest] is not done everyday. Jason would not be able to handle knowing that his uncle is also his father. No kid could handle that. That condition is unacceptable in this world and I wouldn't want it to be acceptable." Carol wondered how she could expect Jason to understand when she could not understand herself. She said, "I can't see destroying Jason's life. The whole thing is a 'box of worms' as my mother would say. But Jason is fully accepted here. We love him. Missy dotes on him; to her he is just a big Cabbage Patch doll." Carol bragged about Jason being "spoiled" by the amount of attention he got from the family.

JAMES'S CONCERNS ABOUT HIS SON

When Jimmy became old enough to babysit for his sisters, James and Carol took advantage of his presence and began to enjoy more freedom. They had an arrangement with Jimmy that he could go roller skating or out somewhere with his friends on Friday night, if he would babysit on Saturday. They paid him for babysitting; in fact, he earned the motorcycle that was to be his as soon as he was legally old enough to drive it. For the first time, James and Carol began to have a social life. James joined a local club, which he called a "drinking club," and found he enjoyed making adult friends and having the opportunity to socialize. His business was doing well, and he felt that he and Carol deserved to have some fun. Their outings usually involved some form of drinking, and James said that he often came home drunk. For the most part Carol accompanied him on these outings. According to James, "For me and Carol to ride through town on the motorcycle and go to a bar on the weekend really makes the rest of the week worthwhile." They both enjoyed their chance to go out and "have some fun" together after many years of remaining at home. After all, they were only in their mid-thirties.

In retrospect, James felt guilty about these good times because he believed he shirked his family responsibility and created the situation that resulted in Darla's pregnancy. He now knows that Jimmy was not responsible enough to care for his sisters, and that the whole family will pay for their mistake the rest of their lives. Additionally, James feels that he was drinking too heavily at that time and that it "took an incident" such as Darla's pregnancy to make him come to that realization.

James said that he did not believe Prosecutor Bettendorf when he first called with the evidence against Jimmy from the blood tests. He admitted that his skepticism was due to his "generally suspicious nature"; that he was inclined to believe that Bettendorf was trying to frame his son. James's sister, Denise, had been married to a man named Bettendorf, the same surname as the local Prosecuting Attorney. Although both Bettendorfs were born and raised in the same town, James denies that they are anything more than distantly related, saying, "There are a whole bunch of Bettendorfs there—the town is full of Germans." When asked if Prosecutor Bettendorf was aware of the fact that James's sister's ex-husband was a Bettendorf, James said, "Sure, he knows Denise." James then looked a little embarrassed and added, "Denise has had to go to court over child support payments from her ex-husband."

James felt that Bettendorf was motivated to falsely accuse Jimmy because Judge Handly was "on Bettendorf's back" to find the perpetrator. James believed that Handly had been genuinely affected by Darla's case at the sterilization hearing. He had met Darla in her eighth month of pregnancy, had viewed tapes of her from the Clay Center, and had listened to the testimony very intently. If Bettendorf could submit evidence against Jimmy, then the case could be dropped. Otherwise, he would have to give blood tests to "half the neighborhood," which would get everyone mad and Bettendorf might lose his job. Charges tend not to be pressed in family situations, so with Jimmy as the perpetrator, Bettendorf would have an easy way out.

James was so tense about the situation that he requested that a Mapleton lawyer tell Bettendorf that James would "blow his brains out all over the office" if he found out that Bettendorf was lying about the paternity test results. James chuckled when he recalled the lawyer's response: "He thought that I was a radical and stupid as hell, but I told him that I was taking control." At the same time, James took Jimmy up to Capital City to have a lie detector test, which Jimmy "passed with flying colors." James talked to people to find out how blood tests could be tampered with. In all, James claimed that he paid over $2,500 for blood tests, lie detector tests, and lawyers to prove that his son was not involved.

In contrast to the mainly positive images of James among Clay Center staff, Dr. Hunt classified him as "belligerent" and "rednecked." When the family arrived for the scheduled blood tests, Hunt claimed that James threatened to "kill" her if she divulged the results to anyone other than himself or Carol. He also specified that he did not want to hear the test results over the telephone or through the mail and indicated that they would come in person to pick up the lab report. Eventually, since it turned out to be inconvenient for them to pick up the test results, they asked Hunt to send them by registered mail. Hunt maintained that everyone on the whole wing of the Newborn Follow-Up Unit was aware of Mr. Helm's presence and he made a lasting impression on them. When they were at the hospital, James "fired off" a number of questions about the meaning and accuracy of the blood tests. Hunt felt that his motive was to get the ammunition to fight the evidence against Jimmy given by Bettendorf. Hunt had the distinct impression that James was not interested in the actual results of the tests or really finding out whether Jimmy had fathered the baby. She asserted that he did not even think that it was wrong for Jimmy to have had sexual intercourse with his sister, but he simply did not want to lose a family battle with his local welfare and legal authorities.

James confessed to having trouble controlling his temper during the past year—a problem he had as a teenager but later overcame. The "stress of the situation" had caused him to "lose control." James felt that if "another kid" had been responsible for the pregnancy, James would have demanded that the prosecuting attorney press charges. He felt that individuals should learn that you have to "pay" when you do something wrong. If he had discovered that it was an older man, James asserted, "I would have had to load my gun."

By the time Jimmy admitted to having had sexual intercourse with Darla, James said he was already convinced that this was the case. Nevertheless, the day Carol gave him the news that the independent blood tests had confirmed Jimmy's paternity of Jason, and that Jimmy had finally confessed his guilt, James "hit the ceiling." He "blew off" at Jimmy for about 3 hours. He claimed that he did not hit Jimmy, but that he has a vile mouth and called his son every possible name he could think of. He summarized that he "drove the point home pretty good."

It was exactly a year from the time Darla's pregnancy was discovered to the time Jimmy confessed. James believed that it was fear of his parents' reaction that caused Jimmy to lie about his incestuous relationship for so long. He speculated that it was also shame and a desire to maintain his family's respect that motivated Jimmy to conceal his guilt and deny the evidence against him. When the prosecuting attorney called to report the results of the first blood tests, Jimmy vehemently denied his guilt. According to James, "Jimmy has good survival instincts and is not below average in intelligence." Jimmy tried to convince his parents of the possibility of a number of other likely culprits.

Jimmy had always been given a good deal of responsibility for Darla. He had to "play nicely" with her and watch her when his mother was busy or out in the yard. James did not feel guilty about imposing these responsibilities on Jimmy nor did he believe that Jimmy resented his parents or sister because of them. In contrast to James's own upbringing, he felt that Jimmy had been indulged. Jimmy had been able to have friends over and was allowed to go roller skating and bowling regularly. He was even permitted to spend the night at friends' homes, an activity that James basically disapproved of because he felt that the boys got into boasting about sex or watching inappropriate shows on television that gave Jimmy ideas. Whereas James had not had many toys as a child, "Jimmy got everything he ever asked for." James felt that he had "gone overboard" in indulging his son because he personally had felt deprived as a child. Jimmy was getting all the things that James had never had. According to James, "Jimmy was on a pedestal in this house. We went out of our way to make the kid happy. He had every darn toy. Maybe it went to his head!"

It might be remembered that Carol's views of Jimmy's childhood were somewhat different. Although both agreed that Jimmy was indulged with material objects, Carol believed that Darla influenced Jimmy's ability to interact normally with his peers, and that Jimmy suffered socially because of Darla. Carol also felt that Jimmy had been deprived of some of the family outings that other children enjoyed. At a later point, James admitted that he and Carol had been "possessed" with finding help for Darla, and that Jimmy was "forced to be the oldest child" and "stay in the background." The father agreed that Jimmy had been taught that his own needs were trivial in comparison to those of his autistic sister. Finally, James admitted that it might not have been the easiest childhood for his son.

James several times emphasized that he was confused about why Jimmy had sexual relations with Darla, but believed that "plenty of thought" went into the act and suspected that it was not a spontaneous, one-time thing. Eventually Jimmy confessed to engaging in sexual intercourse with Darla on numerous occasions over many months. James surmised that it started with watching Darla undress while Jimmy masturbated, and progressed to touching and eventually to intercourse. After trying it, he liked it, and feelings of guilt were not strong enough to stop him. James also assumed that Darla was a willing participant, but said that was irrelevant. Sexual interactions between brother and sister, in James's view, had to be Jimmy's fault, because he was the only one with the intelligence to be potentially responsible. James acknowledged that Darla's behavior could be sexually arousing, but felt that this was not germane to their particular situation. Jimmy had abused their trust. He had failed to be their perfect son. James agonized, "There were 15,000 girls in this town waiting for him. Why didn't he go that route? I'm not so sure he hasn't done that too. He said he hasn't, but who can believe what he says now."

James felt that Jimmy had been taught "right from wrong about sex," and that he was relatively well-informed about sex for a 14-year-old. As James said, "Jimmy was made to put up with my lectures about responsibility, and he seemed to listen and learn." Jimmy never denied that he knew that sexual intercourse could result in pregnancy. When it was pointed out that parents often think they have educated their children when they haven't, or assume that their children are more knowledgeable about sex than they actually are, James vehemently denied that such was the case with Jimmy. James said they had often discussed the sexual content in shows on television. Jimmy had frequently accompanied James to work at the machine shop and had listened to the men's dirty jokes, which James had patiently explained to Jimmy. In James's opinion, Jimmy's actions were inexcusable and unexplainable.

James maintained that his instinct had detected "something wrong" with Jimmy a couple of years before Darla became pregnant. Although unable to clarify the precise nature of his intuition, James described it as "a certain weakness," as "getting too big for his britches," and as a "fascination with adults, particularly women." When given a chance, "Jimmy had jumped into adult conversations." James felt that Jimmy did not have a "moral concept," but would have to show indications of a moral concept before being allowed more freedom to be around girls his age.

James volunteered that he did not know whether the problem that he noticed with Jimmy was Jimmy's or his own, remarking, "I may be the one that is full of crap!" He theorized that a son's sexual development is a threat to a father and said that he was unsure whether some of his hunches were based on a jealous reaction to his son's becoming a good-looking adolescent. James tried to remember the name of what he called "the well-known complex" (the Oedipus complex) that related to this situation and was pleased that the interviewer could name it. During the interviews, James used a number of psychiatric terms (e.g., manic depressive, paranoid, repressed) comfortably and accurately.

James maintained that Carol did not share his perceptions of their son, perhaps because she was a woman or, as a mother, she "tended to protect Jimmy." For similar reasons, James had requested that Jimmy be reassigned to a male therapist at the Mental Health Center. James praised Nancy, admitting that she was shrewd and had a hard, no-nonsense approach—"did not let Jimmy get away with anything." Nevertheless, she "did not have the perceptions of a man"—she was "missing something." James felt that a male therapist would "better understand male drives and feelings" and would "be more likely to be firm about the morality and responsibility appropriate for a man." A man might convince Jimmy "to get control over his sexual drives" and say, "Kid, you screwed up, now how are you going to pay for it?" James also hinted that a male might be less likely to be charmed and manipulated by his attractive son.

James felt that there are presently "too many outs" for people—that "they don't have to pay for their wrongdoing." He believed that a tolerant attitude toward offenders encouraged people to do wrong. He offered as an example that often when a rape occurred it was the woman who was blamed. James did not believe in the legitimacy of excuses for bad behavior. He accused Jimmy of trying to "breeze through the situation" and "underestimate the importance of his act." He felt that Jimmy was avoiding facing his problems and was trying to forget everything and have others forget as well—to pretend that nothing happened. James wanted Jimmy to realize that you cannot make a mistake and just walk away from it. As James put it, "This kind of mistake lasts a lifetime."

James made sure that Jimmy lost a number of privileges and insisted that Jimmy share in caring for Jason. He made Jimmy get up with Jason at night and come home after school to help with the baby. Carol did not agree with this approach. She wanted Jimmy to interact with Jason as a brother or uncle and not as a father. Carol did not want Jason, or anyone else, to know Jimmy was his father.

James and Carol also argued about what James should be called by Jason. Carol had fluctuated between "Grandma" and "Ma" for herself, and settled on "Ma." She wanted James to be called "Dad," but he thought he should be "Grandpa" or, at least, "Pa." Once when Carol handed Jason to James and said, "Go to Daddy," James pointed at Jimmy and said, "You mean him; I'm Grandpa!" This might have been a joke, but nobody in the family found it funny. In an attempt to get James to settle on a name that Jason will call him, when she hands Jason to James, she says, "Here, go to the Thing." James described his wife's nickname for him in a somewhat amused fashion, but seemed genuinely confused about his role in relationship to Darla's child. James felt strongly that he should not be called "Daddy," even though he agreed to take Jason home from the hospital and to raise him as a son. (One has the impression that James felt some discomfort that others might think he is the father of Darla's baby.) He also was indecisive about Jimmy's role. On the one hand, he wanted Jimmy to have responsibility for Jason, yet he did not want Jason to know that he was the consequence of incest.

Although James spoke quite objectively about the situation between Jimmy and himself to an outsider, apparently such was not the case at home. He admitted that he had not said six words to Jimmy during the past 3 months; that his sole interaction with his son was to direct him to his responsibilities around the trailer. James described it as "living in the same house, but not acknowledging each other's existence." Prior to his confession, Jimmy had always accompanied his dad to the machine shop whenever there was an opportunity, but James had not let him come since the paternity was certain.

An exception to the nonrecognition of his son was one Saturday in December when the sun was shining and James just felt like getting out of the house. He got his gun and asked Jimmy if he wanted to go hunting. The boy readily agreed. James had been moody that morning, and when Carol saw the gun she looked at James in alarm. James said, "Carol, I'm not going to shoot him." Again, what might have been a joking comment was not amusing because of the intensity of conflict and emotion in the family. James said that Carol was relieved when they returned from the hunting trip.

James stuck rigidly to his decision to deny his son all privileges. In November, Carol asked James if Jimmy could go to a dance at the high school. James refused to let him go, although he knew Carol was annoyed at his decision. James felt that Jimmy did not need to associate with girls at a dance just then, remarking that, "Kids his age fantasize a lot and I don't think he can deal with his fantasies yet. He is not ready to be turned loose yet. He needs restraints." Then he added, "I won't rest until I find out why he did it."

James stated that Carol and others felt that he continued to punish Jimmy because of personal anger at the boy, but he claimed other motives as well. He conjectured that if Jimmy did not suffer now and "pay for his crime," his guilt would stay with him and he would pay later. James feared that Jimmy might carry his shame into adulthood and it would resurface and interfere with his life at a time when he should have come to peace with himself. James felt that lingering guilt feelings would have a negative impact on Jimmy's ability to be a good husband and father. James believed that only if Jimmy was thoroughly and severely punished would he be able to get over feelings of guilt and shame. James also was convinced that if Jimmy didn't realize his error he might be irresponsible about sex in other situations. James predicted that with the right therapy Jimmy would "turn out all right." James believed that Jimmy was ashamed and did not want his friends to know what happened, although James was obviously agitated when he suggested the possibility of an alternative hypothesis—that Jimmy might have been boasting about his exploits with his sister to his buddies all along. In spite of the fact that Winthrop is a small town, James, like Carol, did not appear very worried that others might find out about family circumstances.

Although Carol thought that Jimmy probably would go to college, James said he did not expect or want his son to go, even though he felt that Jimmy would probably do well there. James talked about his views of the college scene and asserted that college was not important except in cases where someone wanted to become a professional. James said, "Parents pay for college and kids just go to have a good time." James believed that people are (and should be) wild and crazy when they are between the ages of 18 and 22, so he concluded that is the worst time for them to attend college. He argued that most students spend their time in college partying rather than learning. In addition, James felt that colleges require students to take too many irrelevant courses (those not in their area of specialization). It seemed silly to him that a doctor or nurse had to take history or English courses. He added that even courses in a person's major are not always up-to-date and practical. James boasted that he could teach someone more about machines in 10 weeks than a person could learn in 10 years in engineering school. He also said that he would rather hire an employee with real job experience than one with college training.

James acknowledged that Jimmy had good mechanical abilities and enjoyed working with machines. Additionally, Jimmy had benefited from learning from his dad for many years. James said that he might support Jimmy if he wanted to go to a good trade school, but it "would have to be a good one." On the other hand, James said that the last thing he wanted Jimmy to do was to follow in his footsteps. It was clear that James loved machines and his work, and he maintained that he would run the machine shop until he retired, but he did not want Jimmy to work for him. James wanted Jimmy to get out on his own after high school.

While being interviewed, James almost never spontaneously brought up Darla and never once mentioned 6-year-old Missy, but talked mainly of Jimmy and himself and occasionally Carol. When asked about Missy's perceptions of the situation and how she was handling it, James nervously replied that he did not think that she understood anything yet. He dismissed the topic by saying, "We'll cross that bridge when we come to it." Dr. Hunt, the pediatric specialist, was the mother of two young daughters about Missy's age, and she expressed considerable concern about what Missy was witnessing and over-hearing. She also felt that probably nobody was directly explaining the situation to Missy. She worried about the impact on Missy of all that was going on around her. Perhaps James and Carol had too many other problems to think much about their young daughter.

Both Carol and James suggested that Jimmy be interviewed, but because of his age and the nature of the situation, the authors declined the offer. Clearly, his perspective is very relevant to the story, but the authors concluded that his emotional well-being should come first.

CONJECTURE ABOUT THE "PERPETRATOR"

Immediately after they learned Darla was pregnant, people expressed curiosity and anger about the paternity of Darla's baby. This consternation remained evident in those interviewed days, weeks, and months later. Most interviews were conducted while Jason's paternity remained unknown.

Views of the Clay Center Staff

Some Clay staff were very open about their curiosity, their speculations, and their concerns about the paternity of Darla's baby. Teresa Bellows's reaction was typical.

> I was furious at whoever had done it—to take advantage of a low-functioning, nonverbal person—I wanted him arrested instantly and taken away. We were all angry with who had done it, saying things like, "String him up." It was a relief to hear that she was 3 to 4 months pregnant and that it had not happened at the Clay Center. I tried to figure out where someone could have had access to her. It had to have been someone in the family. A nurse at the family planning agency said the sex had probably not been a one-time thing. Again, that pointed to the family.
>
> When I was at the hospital the day after Jason was born, the family members were mixed about whether the paternity was in the family. Carol remarked, "I just wish we knew who did this to her." She was open about it. Carol was a vehement defender of James. She said, "I don't know why they're doing blood tests; it's definitely not

James." On the other hand, Dot filled us in on a lot of things. Dot told us that the doctor said that it might be James. Dot felt there was a strong possibility that it was James. When she found out the baby was blond she said, "Well, James's sister is blond." We knew she was wondering, but it didn't show in the way she acted toward James. She acted warmly toward him.

I observed the men go for the blood tests. They were joking and laughing, saying, "Let's get this over with." But you could observe the tension. Personally, I don't know if it's James's baby. I don't want to pin it on him because Carol likes him. But it has to be a member of the family and I wouldn't blame Jimmy.

Other Clay staff felt it was "unprofessional to speculate." Bill Peterson's reaction was guarded.

We were so into dealing with Darla that those of us in the classroom did not talk much about "who did it." I've been unconcerned with who did it and resented other people speculating. I felt they should not have said things out loud. To assume someone is guilty and say so is unfair . . . unprofessional. At the hospital I knew Carol was thinking about what paternity would mean to her family. She wanted to believe that neither James nor Jimmy was the father of Darla's baby.

A male home programmer said, "Others felt strongly that it was incest. I was trying to reserve judgment. Morrow encouraged openness but told us to put a stop to rumors." Pam Brookshire remarked, "I don't feel like it's my business, really. Why falsely accuse somebody?"

Similarly, Kelly Fincher said, "I felt that we had no right to suspect the father. Information on incest was handed out by the higher-ups. I objected strongly. But it would be good to pinpoint who did it so they could get help." Yet, even those who objected to speculating about paternity, did speculate. Kelly Fincher later said:

There were only so many possibilities: the father, brother, uncle, someone next door, the brother's friends. At home there were only so many people who had access to her. She's not walking the streets at night. It was likely that she got pregnant in her home. I had no feeling about who it was. It could have been a range of people, but it's less likely to be a stranger. Darla wouldn't let a stranger get close to her.

Many believed that the perpetrator could not have been a stranger. As a residential assistant said:

What kind of "sick" would want to have intercourse with her? Knowing her makes it sick, hard to take! To think that humans are capable of that behavior. I'm convinced it has to be someone very close to her. She would attack someone off the street—she would scare them. Darla needs constant supervision. She is only left with family members and close friends. So it is evident that it has to be one of them.

James was most frequently pinpointed as the guilty party. As Brad Parley admitted:

My boss said, "Don't play guessing games about the father," but we did. Fairly early on people assumed it was the father. We thought, "Who else could it be?" Darla's father did not allow her mother to come to the Clay Center alone. It was as if he wanted to keep control of her. I've met them now and they seem so nice, yet I can't figure out who else could have done it. James fed the baby. He was so loving. I've heard, if the baby is born out of incest, then the family can't keep it. So, I wonder what will happen.

Lisa McNeil, who had reminded others not to speculate, had ideas of her own.

My first reaction was "Oh my God, how could anyone do that to her!" My second reaction was that I thought it was her dad. He was the most immediate male in the family. I had seen James in passing. He was the only male in the family I knew about. There was mutual consensus that the dad did it—that was everyone's perception.

Later McNeil said:

I was a little fed up with people trying to imply things that they didn't know—to put blame on others. I was a little upset that qualified staff should so openly assume that the dad did it. I visited the Helms in Winthrop when Darla was home during the last month of her pregnancy. The family were going through the motions of a happy family, but things were strained. Having talked with James, whether he did it or not, I also think that he's a good father. He's very concerned about Darla. It's one of the three (I haven't met the uncle). I hope it's not Jimmy. He already seemed strained. If it is Jimmy, he's gotten some flack already. He'll have a lot more problems than he already has. It's difficult living with Darla. I think if James is guilty he'll stay in the trailer even though Carol said he would not be able to stay.

Teresa Bellows said, "I actually felt it was the father. I knew the parents were concerned about abuse here. I thought the father was using that as a cover-up—that he had been the one to abuse her and was trying to blame it on us. I was upset when Darla's parents took her home." Brad Parley had similar thoughts: "I was thinking that the family probably knew who did this— that probably the father and brother were involved. I was scared they might take her out of state to avoid prosecution." The program secretary simply stated, "Someone in that family needs help more than Darla does!"

Cindy McCormick, who had the most contact with the Helm family, stated:

> Carol most often said that it was neighborhood boys. When she went to the store Darla was left with Jimmy and his friends. She suspected them. She fleetingly said that she had to consider that it might be her husband. She said that if it was her husband, she would make sure he would no longer be in the home.
>
> In a telephone conversation on June 28th she said that the blood tests had cleared two people, but that one was still a possibility. She was extremely upset. No one appeared to have confessed. Carol seemed genuinely concerned. She acted like she did not know who fathered Jason. It did not seem like she was putting on a act to cover for somebody.
>
> I thought that it was the father. I was suspicious of his extreme behavior: First he was very angry, wanting to be in charge, then overly passive (after the court hearing). He had the best access. It seemed that it had to be someone in the family. The brother seemed young. The uncle . . . he's a possibility. But James and Carol have tried a number of things with Darla to try to change her. They have gotten her drunk, had her hypnotized. Possibly they thought that sex, or pregnancy, would have an impact, would be a cure. I have the impression that the sexual behavior has been going on for a while.

Margie Jasper felt that Carol suspected her husband.

> Fairly early on Carol mentioned incest and said she wanted tests carried out to show her husband and son were innocent. But sometimes she acted like she suspected her husband. We felt that she might know more than she had said. We thought that if we could talk to her alone she might reveal her real thoughts about the situation. But it seemed like we only saw her when James was around. She did not have a chance to talk to us privately. In November, at the conference down in Winthrop, James cursed and threatened to "get the pervert

who did it" to his daughter, whereas Carol's concern was Darla. At the conference, when the decision was being made about whether Darla was to return to the Clay program, Carol pleaded, "Don't you understand that my daughter has been raped and you're trying to deny her an education for that reason."

Jasper also described the Helms' visit to Dr. Hanes, the obstetrician who was to deliver Darla's baby if she went into labor before she left the Clay Center at the end of February.

> Dr. Hanes mentioned that he had been in touch with her other doctor, Dr. Franklin, about the case. They discussed the method of delivery and the sterilization decision that the Helms had to make. When Dr. Hanes examined Darla and only Carol and the nurse were in the room, Carol talked openly with the doctor, admitting that, if the father of Darla's baby was her husband or her son, she wanted to know for the sake of her other daughter. The doctor explained that he understood how a loving relationship could become a sexual one. After this encounter with the Helms he remarked to me that he "knew who the father was."

Jasper felt that the family dealt with the paternity issues with denial and that if a family member was responsible, "Carol will have to decide what to do, yet she is not independent enough to make decisions. Dot, Carol's mother, appears to be loyal to James. What Carol does might depend on Dot. I think there is a great possibility of separation or divorce. The results of the paternity investigation might have real ramifications for Darla."

Sandra Werner had thoughts about why the father might have "done it."

> I assumed it was Darla's father. I thought maybe he had the desire to develop a relationship with Darla. It probably started with fondling and when she responded favorably it went further. I thought maybe I could understand how it happened. I also assumed that Darla's mother knew what was going on and condoned it. They did it to have a relationship with Darla. It was founded on their need for responsiveness from Darla. Perhaps the youngster was also seeking physical pleasure, and the parents did not know where to draw the line about what is invasive. I saw a television program on child molesting, and there were men interviewed who sincerely believed that "sex after eight is too late." They felt it was their duty to introduce sex to young kids. Regarding Darla, I think it is best if it happened with the consent of both parents rather than just being the father. That they saw it

as "therapy," rather than just "taking advantage." It's tragic for parents of handicapped children who can't get a reaction out of their kids. I can see why they might try anything.

Nurhan Tokar was the only one who did not suspect Darla's father of being the perpetrator: "I thought to myself, 'What kind of cruel person is making Darla go through this experience?' I suspected the brother. I don't think a father could do it, unless he was deranged."

Views of Community Professionals

During their interviews, most professionals expressed an animated curiosity about the perpetrator. A few were more hushed, conveying a sense of guilt about their interest, as if it was at odds with professional distance and objectivity. Carl Laidlaw believed that "unless Darla wanted to have intercourse, no one could have had intercourse with her. Whatever the case, she did not give verbal consent and she was 15 years old; therefore she was raped. Carol and James want to know the child's paternity. They are angry." Judge Handly also called it "rape," which he defined as "illicit intercourse without consent," and he made sure that it had been reported to the prosecuting attorney. Perhaps because they know the law and are afraid of a libel suit, none of the attorneys volunteered their hunches about the paternity of the baby, except for Laidlaw's suggestion that it had to be someone Darla wanted to have intercourse with. Andrew Edge was not specific when he commented:

> Darla was only left with people Carol trusted. It must have happened right under her nose. I had no indication of sexual abuse in the home before Carol called to say Darla was pregnant. I don't think Carol had any inkling that Darla was pregnant before the Clay people called her. When she called us to make an appointment, she blamed Clay staff for the pregnancy.

Many Winthrop and Mapleton people stated outright that James Helm was the guilty one. Fred Quail said:

> I have my own feelings. I think it's the father. I would take bets on it. My hunch just comes from talking with him, little things. If that had been my daughter, I'd be pursuing it as hard as I could and he isn't. I asked Ken Ingalls and he said the same thing. That mother did not leave Darla alone with anyone. She was the most overprotective parent I know.

Ken Ingalls hypothesized:

You wouldn't really expect Darla to relate to somebody else. As strong
as she is, she would push somebody away and resist. When Darla did
not want to walk down the hall at school, for example, she lay down
on the floor and it took six people to get her up. I feel that it had to be
somebody Darla or the family knew. It's unrealistic to think she'd
been raped by an outsider. I took a paper to the trailer for Carol to
sign to return to the Clay Center. James was not home. I had coffee
with Carol. She said, "If it's somebody I know, that person will not
come in this house again." She said it calmly over coffee. She was
speaking rationally, although she is very upset about the situation. It's
a difficult pill for Carol to swallow.

When she heard from Ken Ingalls that Darla was pregnant, Elise Yoder
assumed that it had happened at the Clay Center. She felt guilty because she
had encouraged the Helms to send Darla there, and she hoped that the Helms
would not blame her for influencing their decision. Later, when she found
out the pregnancy happened before Darla went to Clay, Yoder said:

When I first heard, my initial reaction was that it was an outsider because of what Carol had told me had happened a couple of years ago.
But when I got to thinking about it, I began to suspect Jimmy. I felt
that Darla always came first in that family and that Jimmy probably
resented that. He was embarrassed about Darla, so the Helms moved
him to another school. They didn't move Darla even though we were
trying to get them to allow her to be sent to the severe/profound program close by. Carol bragged that Jimmy could handle Darla. I always
thought that was too much responsibility, but I never told Carol that I
felt that way. I wish that I had though.

In Mapleton, Thomas Franklin said: "I thought about the perpetrator. I
couldn't imagine a stranger being accepted by her. I thought incest was likely."
Jana Jones, obstetrical nurse, elaborated:

When I met the parents on the way to surgery I was introduced to
Darla, James, Carol, and Dot. I suspected that the child abuse had
occurred in the family. I knew it had to be someone in close contact
with Darla. I thought about the father right off. He was too sweet, too
nice, too well-mannered, too helpful—a little bit too much. It seemed
like an act. The father was the only one who was able to get Darla into

a wheelchair. I wondered why the father had more power over her than the mother. Usually the mother is the caregiver and the one with control. But I didn't get the feeling from the mother that she suspected her husband. They were warm and affectionate with each other. If it had been me, I would have been cold and suspicious until I knew for sure that it was not my husband. It would have interfered with my relationship. I thought, "Maybe she's covering," "maybe she's so stupid she doesn't suspect." I was bothered. I would deal right now with "who did this" if it were my daughter. I could not live with not knowing for several months. I would force a confession out of who did it and never see them again.

In the afternoon Darla's uncle and brother arrived. I immediately made a judgment on the uncle. I found myself judging—I knew I shouldn't have! I also found myself stereotyping. I suspected the uncle because of his physical appearance. He was a big, burly guy with an unkempt appearance and a gruff manner. He had a hard look, like he was into motorcycles. He had key chains on him and a smirky appearance. I know I should know better but I couldn't help it. I suspected him and I did not like him. Also, when I went to check Darla's incision and change the dressing, he moved over to see. I didn't care about other family members seeing, but I resented his coming to see. So I did the work under the sheet. I wouldn't expose Darla to her uncle. I did not think that it was his place to see his niece naked. It was too familiar. At that point I did not know that he was there for the blood test. When I found that out, I was even more suspicious. I couldn't understand why everyone else was being friendly to him.

I did not suspect the little brother. He just sat there quietly. I thought the sexual relationship had to be with someone over a long time period and he was just 14 years old. He was just getting into hormones and sex drive. He wasn't even a big 14-year-old. Darla was bigger than him. She probably would have resisted, and her brother would not have had the physical strength to coerce her.

Without ever observing the family together, State Department of Education Consultant Susan Andrews, a respected authority on child abuse, stated her belief that the perpetrator was in the immediate or extended family. She knew close supervision of Darla was needed and strangers would be unlikely to have access to her. The family's concern about sex was an indication that their environment might be sexually charged. The large number of adult males living in or "frequenting" the small space of the trailer created a "high risk" situation for sexual exploitation. Lastly, because Darla is nonverbal and severely retarded she is particularly vulnerable to sexual abuse.

Dr. Hunt categorized the whole family's behavior as "sexually aberrant," noting that she had been shocked that Carol kissed all of her children on the mouths, even 15-year-old Jimmy. She also quoted Carol as having claimed that they "all slept together anyway" when they stayed in a guest room on the previous visit to the hospital. The parents told Hunt that someone at the Clay Center had raped Darla, but she had already heard from Clay staff that the baby had been conceived prior to Darla's starting at the Center.

Donna Karnes believed that the perpetrator was an "insider." She said that observing Darla's behavior in the home in the presence of the person whom she suspected of paternity, had given her a "notion" of who was responsible. She also conjectured that the sexual intercourse had been a "forceful thing—a case of rape." Karnes was unsure about how the case would be treated. One possibility was that the perpetrator would get a jail sentence, unless there was not enough evidence to convict. Age and intelligence of the perpetrator were factors. Sometimes a 2-year probation was given in the case of a first offense or if there were mitigating circumstances. In other words, the nature of the penalty depended on the nature and extent of abuse and the circumstances of the guilty person. If the victim or the victim's family does not press charges, then therapy is an option. In some cases the suspect agrees to undergo therapy if the family does not press charges. Karnes said that she was interested in determining who did it so that person "could get the help he needs," because "anyone who would rape an autistic child really needs help," he would "be a person with real psychiatric problems."

It is interesting that James was not aware of others' suspicions of him, especially since he calls himself "paranoid." Questions about whether others suspected him of paternity were rephrased in different ways and asked several times. James consistently responded that "feeling accused had not been threatening or uncomfortable" for him. He did relate that one man at work had assumed he was the father and had tried to hit James, but after an explanation he quickly believed James's denials. James calmly speculated that people probably suspected him at first but after talking to them for "4 or 5 minutes" he "clarified the situation" and "they understood." He claimed that "Carol never thought it was me." Because James was open about his feelings and told many tales about himself or his family that others might have concealed, it seems that his denials of others' suspicions were sincere. At his first interview, James assured the interviewer that the responsible party was an outsider, probably one of Jimmy's friends.

A variety of evidence suggests that Darla enjoyed sexual stimulation; the surprise in the case was that her brother had the reputation of being "a very good boy" and sexually inexperienced. Because intercourse with Darla was thought of by most of those involved as child sexual abuse, it was assumed that it could have been carried out only by someone terrible, insensitive, or with special power over her. None of these descriptors applied to Darla's younger brother, who seemed gentle and caring, and had looked after her patiently for years. Their play, since it could not be verbal, included much body contact. It is likely that such physical contact evolved into sexual activity usually considered appropriate only for adults, for people without disabilities, and, of course, for individuals outside the family.

Darla had no idea of the codes she was breaking; she could remain innocent in the eyes of the beholders. On the other hand, Jimmy, her brother, was fully cognizant of societal codes but, apparently, could not control his curiosity and temptation. This crisis has passed for Darla, but the ramifications of Jimmy's infraction no doubt will continue throughout his lifetime. Missy also will surely be influenced by the circumstances surrounding the ordeal. How the events affected James and Carol, this chapter has made vividly clear.

CHAPTER 6

Tensions for Professionals

The confirmation of Darla's pregnancy triggered animated philosophical debates among all those involved. People considered varying views of sexual abuse and incest. They attempted to distinguish the rights to sexual expression for people with disabilities versus the need to protect vulnerable individuals from the transgressions of others. They examined how individual needs might conflict with their own views of proper family life. Sadness, anger, fear, and relief accompanied shifts in viewpoints and expansion of beliefs.

CONCERN ABOUT DECISION MAKING

A major problem for professionals at the time of Darla's pregnancy was that they were responsible for her care, but had little or no power to influence the decisions concerning her that were made. A number of participants in Winthrop, in Mapleton, and at the Clay Center were bothered that Darla had to go through with the pregnancy, that she was returned to the Clay Center pregnant, and that she had a C-section instead of a vaginal birth. Some were upset that she had been sterilized. Many worried about Darla's possible continued contact with "the perpetrator." Many were not satisfied with the way the abuse aspects of the case were being handled. Professionals were concerned about who should raise the infant and debated whether the Helms should have had the choice of raising Jason.

Professionals were frustrated that their opinions were not heard—that they were not consulted about decisions. Bill Peterson said, "We had no say-so about the baby. It was hard being responsible for Darla and yet not having the responsibility to make the best decision." A program assistant said:

> As hourly staff, we didn't feel in control. There was a difference of opinion about whether she should have the baby and get her tubes tied. We were concerned about what would happen to the baby. We worried about Darla's sister being in that home. We had a number of

concerns and it was frustrating not to have more power to influence decisions. Nobody asked us, and I guess we wanted them to.

Getting Sterilization Approved

Within a day of learning of Darla's pregnancy, the Helms brought up the idea of sterilization for her. Carol had a tubal ligation when Missy was born, and knew that such surgery was most easily done at the time of delivery. At their first meeting with Dr. Edge, Carol mentioned their interest in sterilization, and she repeated this information in her initial telephone conversation with Dr. Franklin. Franklin immediately informed Carol that he would do a sterilization only if legal permission was obtained.

Sometime during late November or early December, the Helms asked their attorney, Carl Laidlaw, to file a petition to permit Darla's sterilization. Laidlaw had never had a sterilization case before and could not recall one ever happening in Hudson County. Laidlaw had not met Darla, so he requested a meeting at his office. Within 5 minutes of her arrival, Laidlaw concluded that the sterilization request was appropriate.

Laidlaw then asked the Hudson County Judge, Melvin Handly, who was responsible for hearing evidence and deciding on the sterilization, to sign an order for surgical sterilization without a hearing. Judge Handly refused Laidlaw's request. Handly had already heard of Darla's pregnancy from Paul Bettendorf, Hudson Country Prosecuting Attorney, who had been pursuing the sexual abuse charges connected with Darla's pregnancy. Handly's decision not to grant permission for the sterilization without a hearing was based on the fact that Darla was "an underage U.S. citizen operating under a disability"; therefore, he ordered a "full-blown hearing." Looking back, he thought this might have been "making a mountain out of a molehill," but his first response was that sterilization was so invasive and radical that it required a hearing.

Judge Handly then appointed a young lawyer, Richard Vaughn, Guardian ad Litem for Darla. A Guardian ad Litem is frequently appointed in cases involving individuals who are considered incompetent in looking out for their own best interests, such as juveniles, the elderly, and people with disabilities. Vaughn had grown up in Winthrop. After receiving his law degree in a neighboring state, Vaughn returned to Winthrop where he had practiced law for almost 3 years. Vaughn had acted as Guardian ad Litem two or three times before in juvenile matters, but not on behalf of anyone with disabilities. The other cases also did not involve sterilization. Vaughn claimed no special competencies for the role of Guardian and said the position was simply rotated among all members of the Hudson County Bar.

Vaughn met Darla and her parents in Laidlaw's office. He apparently walked into the conference room, sat down, and introduced himself to Darla. Darla's response was to scream and hit her head with the palm of her hand. Laidlaw, who was present during this encounter, recalled: "Vaughn went white as a sheet and had to leave the room. She really got to him." Although Vaughn admitted that both Laidlaw and Carol Helm had described Darla, he had not expected the "loudness" and "violence." He had been "caught by surprise." Darla eventually settled down and paced the room without screaming. After that first meeting, Vaughn remarked to Laidlaw, and later repeated to Judge Handly, "If ever there was a case for sterilization, Darla was it." Vaughn's "heart went out to the family" and he "admired what they were doing," sensing that "they cared about Darla."

Dr. Franklin was subpoenaed to appear in Hudson County Court for the February 20 sterilization hearing. He was asked to give an opinion on the medical risks of tubal ligation performed immediately after childbirth, the advantages of sterilization over other forms of contraception, and Darla's ability to bear a normal child. Franklin told Handly that the most convenient time for the tubal ligation was immediately following childbirth. He also indicated that sterilization was the safest and most effective birth control method for someone who did not ever want to have a child. He informed the court that due to Darla's condition, sterilization was likely to be the only effective form of birth control. Franklin felt Darla's chances of bearing a normal child were slim because her bizarre eating habits were likely to result in nutritional inadequacies or the introduction of toxic substances into the fetus' system. The possibility of incest and her own autistic condition also increased the risks for handicapped offspring. When he was questioned about the decision to allow her pregnancy to continue, Franklin told Judge Handly that by the time Darla became his patient she was almost 6 months pregnant and it was too late to perform an abortion. The trip to Winthrop and the court hearing took most of Franklin's day. The court experience was stressful for Franklin, and he was glad to leave when his testimony was over.

Judge Handly began talking about his role by stating that "dealing with this sort of case was hard, painful—that one had to immerse oneself temporarily and then forget about it." Yet his recollection of details of the hearing made it clear that he had not forgotten much about this case. Handly met Darla only once, when she accompanied her parents into the court on the day of her sterilization hearing. Darla's screaming and disruptive restlessness caused Handly to comment, a few minutes after the hearing commenced, "I've seen enough," and he dismissed her from the courtroom. Videotapes of Darla were shown by Clay Center staff at later points in the hearing. Although Handly had previously dealt with petitions for guardianship for a number of people who were nonverbal or verbally limited, Darla was the first person with autism he had ever met.

Melvin Handly described a judge as having two entities: one personal and one professional. In making decisions in court, the personal is suppressed. Handly tried to ignore anything that was not presented in the courtroom— what he referred to as "rumors" he had heard relating to the case and the involved individuals. In connection with Darla's sterilization decision, rumors included the "criminal problem," the fact that a rape had been committed. He defined rape as "illicit intercourse without consent," and said that he considered Darla to have been raped because she was not capable of consent. Handly ignored these separate issues and focused on evidence related directly to the sterilization decision. However, Handly said that after the hearing he reported the rape to Bettendorf, as he knew the Department of Public Welfare and the police had done before. Handly asked himself a number of questions in weighing evidence, including the qualifications of those testifying, the motives of the parties involved, and the validity of the evidence. Handly looked for "signs of nervousness" in those who testified, which might indicate that a person was lying.

Darla's case was the first and only sterilization decision for Handly and for the Hudson County Court. Handly credited the Clay Center staff with bringing a "good deal of evidence" (testimony and videotapes) that was "exceptionally helpful" because he wanted "overkill" in this case. Clay staff present at the hearing described Judge Handly as very moved, sad, and almost in tears when he concluded:

> After hearing what I have today, and careful consideration, I approve the petition to have Darla Helm sterilized with a tubal litigation. She should not suffer with another pregnancy and there should be no chance that another severely handicapped child be brought into the world.

Handly then added: "I will make sure steps are taken for a full investigation into the paternity of the child." Handly felt that he was correct in deciding for sterilization, even though he is basically opposed to involuntary sterilization because it is an "invasion of a citizen's rights" and hence a "last resort." Handly repeated that once he makes a decision he likes to leave the whole thing behind him and that he would "go nuts" if he had lingering doubts or was unable to forget painful cases.

School Superintendent Quail was annoyed with Judge Handly, with whom he had discussed Darla's case at a party. Quail had apparently asked the judge what was being done about Darla, and Judge Handly replied that "it had been taken care of," a statement that was interpreted by Dr. Quail to mean that Darla had been sterilized. Quail was incensed at Handly's response, claiming that the "legal sloppiness blew his mind." Quail was generally con-

cerned that the "perpetrator of the crime" be apprehended. Quail also volunteered that anything Bettendorf took on had a "90% chance of being botched
up." Further, he asserted that the welfare department "would not pursue the
case any more than the judge or prosecutor wanted."

Clay staff were disappointed with Vaughn at the hearing, accusing him
of not really having Darla's best interests in mind. McCormick complained:
"The Guardian ad Litem was very passive. I felt that he should have been
more involved. He had little information and did not seem to see things from
her side." Others worried that Vaughn was "too influenced" by the Helms'
family lawyer, Carl Laidlaw. They felt that he should have spoken up about
pursuing the sexual abuse aspects of Darla's case. Vaughn felt his role as
Guardian related specifically and solely to the sterilization, and not to broader
concerns for Darla's welfare, such as whether it was in Darla's best interests
to remain in a home where the sexual abuse had probably taken place, or
whether sterilization would encourage further abuse of Darla. Vaughn asserted
that Darla should not "be allowed to remain fertile to catch criminals." He
felt that pregnancy was a "tragic" thing for Darla and quoted Laidlaw as having
said that sterilization "was the only humane thing to do."

Clay Center employees were also disappointed with the role of Protection and Advocacy in Darla's predicament. Mark Johnson, a lawyer who was
the head of the State Protection and Advocacy Commission until shortly after
Jason's birth, was called by Clay Center staff regarding the sterilization and
abuse aspects of Darla's case. His successor, Arno Green, learned about
Darla's situation from Johnson and other commission staff. For a number of
reasons, they were unable to be of much assistance in the case. In the first
place, their roles are fairly narrowly defined, and both Johnson and Green
admitted to being personally confused about how they were to get involved
in cases such as Darla's. The Commission was set up and mandated by federal law to "protect the interests" of individuals with developmental disabilities. Theoretically, Protection and Advocacy was to have "legal" and "philosophical" dimensions; however, in actuality, its legal clout is nonexistent—it
has not been empowered to enforce laws. Moreover, often, as in the case of
sterilization, there is no law to enforce. Lobbying by commission employees,
such as for relevant legislation, was also forbidden. Not only could they not
initiate action, but when their services were requested by outside parties they
could only offer advice. Green had been contacted about a "couple of other
sterilization cases" by "on-lookers," once by a teacher and once by an employee
at a sheltered workshop. He never heard what happened with those cases and
said that people often called him for advice but never kept him informed about
how a case was resolved. He mentioned this rather disinterestedly and did not
go on to state that perhaps the policies of the agency might need modification
if they were to serve people with disabilities and their families.

Both Green and Johnson suspected that sterilization was being done on some people with developmental disabilities in the state; however, they believed that they were not hearing about such cases because it was in the doctors' or parents' interests to avoid contact with their agency. Both felt that most doctors would refuse to perform sterilization surgery on patients with disabilities, due to worry about legal risks. Although Green and Johnson's logic is puzzling, they conjectured that many doctors would be reluctant even if granted permission by the courts because of the Indiana 1978 *Stump v. Sparkman* case. This case involved a 15-year-old "somewhat retarded" girl, Linda Sparkman, who was sterilized in 1971 at the request of her mother. Permission was granted by Circuit Court Judge Stump. Several years later, after she had married and was unsuccessful in becoming pregnant, Sparkman learned of the nature of her surgery. At that point she sued the judge, the surgeon, the hospital, her mother, and her mother's attorney. Because he was acting in his professional capacity, Judge Stump was granted judicial immunity; therefore the other defendants also could not be found liable. Sparkman did not win the suit, so it is unclear why Protection and Advocacy officials felt that this litigation would be a deterrent against performing sterilization surgery.

Mr. Green said that when he is contacted, he recommends "no sterilization" for either children or adults with handicaps. Green said his position had not been directed by the federal government or "higher-ups," but was based on his own recognition of the basic right of all humans to procreate. He said if the woman's life were to be in jeopardy as a result of a pregnancy, he would support sterilization if other forms of birth control were not advisable.

Indiana, the state in which Darla lived, passed a law in 1907 that permitted involuntary sterilization of people with mental retardation and other disabilities. Indiana happened to be the first state to pass such a law, although more than half of the states eventually enacted similar legislation (Burgdorf, 1983). The law was repealed in the 1970s, and nothing was put in its place. Green and Johnson believed that there had been a decline in sterilizations of citizens with disabilities since the law was repealed, but had no real data to back up this hunch. Neither was able to provide any information about the incidence of sterilization petitions within the state because the cases handled in the circuit courts are kept in their local records and are not collected at the state level unless cases are heard in an appellate or state supreme court. Additionally, the information is difficult to obtain from court recorders because it is listed according to the names of the parties involved, and not by topic. Moreover, the records do not include the reasons behind decisions.

Athough Johnson and Green felt that a statute providing guidelines for sterilization was needed, they were not optimistic that one might be enacted. Johnson said:

Legislators, being political, have backed off controversial issues because of a desire not to alienate their constituency. Since it would deal with such a small segment of the population, there was no real incentive for legislators to introduce a bill related to sterilization. Legislators tend to be attuned to large, nonspecific issues in which they can take positions that please voters.

Without an enabling statute (law authorizing sterilization), the legal situation regarding sterilization of people with disabilities is very fuzzy, requiring considerable personal interpretation by local lawyers and judges, and providing no guidance for medical doctors, who, as a result, may not act at all for fear of negative legal repercussions.

Reactions to the Sterilization

There was considerable polarization of opinion among Clay Center staff about Darla's sterilization. The most enthusiastic proponent was a young male program assistant who proudly proclaimed: "I've been sterilized. Obviously I do not have the feeling that sterilized people are not whole people. I'm proud of my vasectomy. It provides freedom. Sure, I'm glad Darla was sterilized. I don't see any problem with it." In contrast, a young female argued, "Sterilization violates her rights as a human." She also reasoned, "I do not want Darla to go through a pregnancy again."

Many were uneasy about the impact Darla's sterility would have on future sexual abuse. McNeil said:

I don't believe they should have sterilized her. I would like to know the reasoning behind it. The "preventive measure" should be Darla's being safe. It makes me angry that they had her sterilized. It makes it easier for them not to worry about Darla. Well, they should worry about Darla—about whether she's safe with people in her environment.

Less decided, Bellows contended:

It should have been done. It would be horrifying if she had to go through a pregnancy again. But it gives the male total freedom. Anyway, the threat of pregnancy was a small barrier to sex. I don't think she should have more kids. I guess I have mixed feelings about it.

Other Clay employees were ambivalent. Peterson said: "It's less than an ideal situation that she needs it. But it was a good idea. Certainly we don't want her to have another baby." Werner said: "If we could be assured that she wouldn't be raped again, there would be no need to do it. But when there is no control, then the operation is essential. She needs to be protected so a pregnancy will never happen again. It's like a Band-Aid on the situation." Brookshire said: "I'm glad for Darla—she'll never have to go through another pregnancy. I really doubt that her parents would take on a third handicapped child. I'm glad for any child's sake that might have been born. But it was not a way to take away more child abuse." Fincher agreed, saying, "A tubal ligation only takes away part of the problem. The sexual abuse will continue." Tokar felt: "It's a good thing in that she's not going to get pregnant again. If it was abuse, sterilization is not going to stop it—it could almost encourage it—but pregnancy is no viable consequence. If she's initiating sexual activity, because that's what she wants to do, then she won't get pregnant." Another residential program assistant said:

> It's the best thing for Darla. She's come from an environment where she's had a lot of sexual intercourse. If she didn't get sterilized a pregnancy would probably happen again. From my position as a mother, I remember being scared about childbirth. I had an easy childbirth—quick—but there still was a lot of work and pain. It changed my life. For a child who doesn't understand, it's cruel to make her go through pregnancy and labor.

Still another remarked:

> I feel fine about the sterilization. Darla doesn't need to be having a bunch of kids. She shouldn't be producing offspring for her family. She shouldn't be in a situation to be pregnant again. She ran into it. It found her. She doesn't need that. I'm not opposed to handicapped people having kids, but there should be a certain functioning level. They should be able to deal with the consequences of having children.

Margie Jasper was present when Carol and James Helm asked Dr. Hanes about having Darla sterilized when her baby was born. She described the scene.

> The doctor would not indicate whether or not he would do it. You could tell he was uncomfortable about being asked. He said that there were legal issues that would prevent him from doing a tubal ligation even if court permission came through. He knew of cases where suits had been brought later not only against the parents and the doctor,

but even against the court for granting permission for a sterilization. Personally, I did not think they would be given legal permission to sterilize Darla. I felt that she should be protected from pregnancy without being sterilized. Realistically, her behavior could be perceived as seductive and she would be vulnerable to abuse; thus there was a high risk for repeated pregnancy. I was torn about all of this. I wanted to protect her from abuse but realized that this might not be realistic for the rest of her life. The doctor brought up the possibility of a hysterectomy. Darla's mother was opposed to that. She felt that a tubal might be more temporary, less invasive. It was all so medically sticky.

I had additional reasons for not wanting Darla to be sterilized. I lived in Mapleton before I came here and my children were born at Southside Hospital. My choice of hospital for Darla was St. Teresa's, which mainly served the high risk babies, but it's a Catholic hospital and they would not allow a sterilization to be performed there. Southside Hospital is an elitist hospital. Public Welfare families there had gotten some harassment on bills. I felt that they would not be understanding with the Helm family. Also, Dr. Franklin was not as familiar with Southside Hospital. He usually worked at St. Teresa's Hospital. I felt that, since the staff was not accustomed to dealing with Dr. Franklin, they might oppose him or not cooperate with him. Looking back, my worries were unnecessary. Southside worked out just fine.

At another point, Jasper recalled: "Dr. Franklin and Dr. Hanes disagreed profoundly in approach. Franklin was willing to do a tubal ligation; Hanes probably would not. I agreed with Hanes." Jasper appeared to confuse a willingness to take chances with the legal system and perform the sterilization operation, with personal approval of such an operation. Actually, Hanes's own stand regarding sterilization of individuals with disabilities is unknown; however, he confessed to worrying about the personal risks of being sued at a later date if he performed the surgery. Franklin thought that a tubal ligation for Darla was appropriate, and he agreed to take the risks and perform the operation.

Perhaps the most poignant statement about sterilization came from Nurhan Tokar, himself the father of two small children.

Given the nature of the autistic population, given her level of development—perhaps they should have done it. On the other hand, you never know in what way she might develop in the future. There's little possibility of her getting married and wanting to have children. I'm familiar with the eugenics movement and how it can be applied to

slow learners and abused, but the reality is that these people [low
functioning people with autism] never return to normalcy and so sterilization is better for them. But the special population has to go
through it because of the fear of the normal population. Special
groups suffer. Darla had no part in it [wanting sexual intercourse] but
she had to suffer because someone else was inhumane.

In any event, there was a consensus among professionals, parents, and
most others who knew Darla that she should not become pregnant again.
Although some believed that sterilization violated her rights, no one who knew
Darla during this period could visualize allowing her to experience another
pregnancy.

Regrets About Abortion

As might be expected, abortion was another highly charged topic. Various
rationales were given for abortion: that a young teenager with disabilities who
had not intended to get pregnant should not be forced to carry a baby for
9 months; that there were serious, perhaps life-threatening, health risks for a
15-year-old; and that the baby's impact on others as well as its own quality of
life might be so unsatisfactory as to make aborting it a better choice. Apparently, when the Helms first heard that Darla was pregnant they both assumed
she would have an abortion. However, they quoted Andrew Edge, their family doctor, as having said that a second trimester abortion was very dangerous, even life-threatening to the mother, and he would not recommend it for
Darla. Edge also told them that second trimester abortions were not legal in
the state. The Helms said that they had received the same information and
advice from other doctors. At the same time, Clay staff and Fran Ellis at the
Clay County family planning clinic recalled having given the family information about clinics in two neighboring states that would perform abortions of
pregnancies of up to 6 months' gestation. Neither Carol nor James recalled
receiving such information. In any case, no abortion was performed.

Although Clay employees' disagreement about whether Darla should
have gone through with the pregnancy tended to reflect the polarized stands
visible in the national debate on abortion, some who claimed to be ambivalent about or opposed to abortion were in favor of abortion in Darla's case.
Parley wavered: "I know the abortion issue was raised. I'm not big on abortion or unwanted children. I really don't know enough to have an opinion
about abortion but I did not want Darla to go through with the pregnancy."
McNeil said: "I didn't think she should be allowed to have the baby. I'm not
pro-abortion, but in a situation like that I thought that abortion was best. I
argued with others about this. Some staff are very pro-life!" Peterson felt:

It seemed logical for her to have an abortion. Most people thought that, regrettably, it would be in her best interest. There were no positive factors about continuing the pregnancy and no alternatives to abortion. No one was expressing "no abortion." I had no opinion. I came the closest to "no abortion" that anyone got.

Peterson's contacts were classroom staff, so he apparently was unaware of the residential staff who opposed abortion.

Many were surprised that Darla did not have an abortion. Werner said:

I wished that she'd had an abortion. I just assumed she'd have an abortion. I was disappointed when they said they wouldn't—probably their decision had religious grounds. Abortion would have been the best way to resolve a difficult situation. It would have been easier on everyone, including the staff. However, I have been rethinking my feelings on abortion. I'm not as much for abortion as I was 6 to 8 months ago. I have begun to question what I thought I knew, what I believed in.

McCormick said: "Carol often talked to me about decisions. I thought they should allow Darla to have an abortion. I worried about her carrying the baby and the condition of the baby. But I didn't think I should push my opinions." Jasper said: "Darla would have had an abortion had she been my child!"

Tokar said: "I thought she should have an abortion rather than force her to bear a child. I felt sorry to have to wake her up to take her to the toilet— it was torture for her. I thought she was too young to have a baby, that her bones were still in the process of development." Bellows said: "Originally we thought she'd have an abortion. We thought it would be automatic because of her condition. We were surprised that she didn't. We didn't think that going full term would be good for Darla. Abortion would have been the best thing all around."

The program secretary, who had just returned from maternity leave, said: "Pregnancy is hard enough when a normal person goes through it. It's not fair for an autistic person who does not want a baby. If there was ever a case for an abortion, this was it." She also favored an abortion because she felt there was no way that Darla's child would be able to lead a normal life because of its parentage. Brookshire also worried about the quality of the future life of Darla's baby, saying: "It was unfair to bring a child into the world without a good home. I pictured it growing up in an institution." A young male program assistant said, "I had serious doubts that Darla would have a normal kid. I didn't want to see her go through 5 more months of the crap—kid kicking and all the other things—and not understanding a thing about it. I did not know who would raise the kid—not Darla! What would it be like for a kid growing up knowing that Darla was his mother?"

Others favored abortion because they suspected that Darla's baby would not be normal. A program assistant said, "I'm not usually pro-abortion, but I was pretty sure this baby would not be normal." Brookshire emotionally stated: "It would have been better for that child to be stillborn. It will probably be profoundly retarded—another wasted life brought into the world." Tudor confessed: "I was in tears when I heard that Darla was going to carry the baby. Later, when I was at the hospital after Jason was born, the Helms were very defensive about Darla's ability to bear a normal child. They tried to deny Jason's condition."

Community professionals questioned why an abortion had not been performed. Fran Ellis maintained: "I gave the Clay staff information about where the Helms could get a late abortion for Darla—names of clinics where abortions are permissible up to 22 and 24 weeks—in locations that are only a couple of hours away from Winthrop. The Clay social worker gave that information to Darla's parents. I was surprised that the family did not choose abortion." Susan Andrews said: "I was concerned whether the parents knew enough to make a correct decision. I was surprised that Darla did not have an abortion." Jana Jones, obstetrical nurse, asserted: "I'm pro-choice. I think an abortion would have been the best for all concerned." Among the few to specifically mention that Darla had passed the first trimester when the pregnancy was discovered, Vaughn said: "I wondered why the baby was not aborted during the second trimester. I was concerned about both Darla and the fetus."

The Meaning of Sexual Expression for Darla

During the interviews, it became clear that some of the attitudes and stereotypes held by professionals about the sexuality of people with disabilities, were as misguided and misleading as those of lay members of the community. A 15-year-old female who is severely retarded and autistic is not expected to be sexually active and perhaps enjoy her sexual experiences. People with disabilities are sexual beings, yet most people who knew or worked with Darla were surprised, shocked, or even disgusted when they first heard of her pregnancy. Interest in the "perpetrator of the sexual abuse" was more prominent than the meaning of all this for Darla.

Many eventually did begin to talk about Darla as a willing participant—even an initiator—of sexual interactions. They began to understand that someone with severe disabilities might still have sexual needs. Jerry Roderick said, "We can't promote sexual activity between our clients but we have to recognize their sexual needs. I guess we have to teach her proper and safe masturbation procedures." Others felt that their roles regarding the sexuality of their clients might be broader than redirecting public masturbation. Felicia Tudor puzzled: "I worry about how we'll deal with Darla's sexual frustration here at the center. Masturbation may not be enough to meet her sexual needs. She seems interested in social/sexual relationships." Fincher said:

> It seems like she likes sex. It's true we call it abuse because she can't consent to it, yet I'm all for the rights of handicapped people. And she seems to have a need for sex. She has an undeniable right to have sex. The question is: Who should she have sex with? A friend of the family? Another student? There have been people throughout the state who think it is terrible to train clients to masturbate. How do we handle the sexual needs of our clients?

Most of the staff felt that Darla's severe retardation made the situation extremely complex. Roderick, however, saw Darla's inability to comprehend the implications and social stigma of her situation as a benefit: "It probably helped that Darla did not understand what was happening. She felt no shame. She did not suspect the abhorrence others felt about the whole situation. A girl of normal intelligence might have suffered more." Whereas Darla was oblivious to the scandal and its repercussions, Jimmy, also a child at the time the incest occurred, would bear the burden, the secret, and the guilt for the rest of his life.

One point made clear by Darla's story is that her sexual drive and capacity for sexual pleasure existed in spite of her autism and retardation. Darla's sexual experience may have been one of the most "normalized" and satisfying experiences of her life to that point. It may even be conjectured that because of the limits to Darla's cognitive life (e.g., she did not read, watch television, or engage in conversations), and her restricted and confined life circumstances, sexual expression is even more important to her than to those of us who have a broader range of sources of personal fulfillment (Brantlinger, 1983, 1988a, 1988b).

Furthermore, Darla continued to live at home through adolescence. These normalized, community experiences are the ones that modern professionals and advocates are encouraging when they speak about normalization and community integration (Alaszewski & Ong, 1990; Wolfensberger, 1972). The challenge then becomes how to provide opportunities for people with autism and mental retardation to become sexually fulfilled and how to evaluate the circumstances that are appropriate for sexual expression. Many have proposed that special sexual arrangements be developed for physically handicapped individuals, including the use of willing prostitutes. Others advocate teaching how to masturbate to achieve orgasm to persons with mental retardation and autism. Impersonal sex and self-stimulation might not be sufficient, however, for those who enjoy sexual expression within a warm and intimate social context.

ALTERED PERCEPTIONS

People who were interviewed in this study admitted that the circumstances of Darla's pregnancy forced them to re-evaluate many of their very basic assumptions. A few who thought they were categorically opposed to abortion or sterilization admitted that they became somewhat less rigid in their stands. Others began to realize that sterilization did not solve all problems. Perhaps the most unsettling themes concerned incest. At the time most of the interviews were conducted, the paternity of Darla's baby had not been established, although most suspected that it was a family member. A number of people felt that after getting to know the Helms, they had less clear-cut opinions about incest. As Werner said:

> I now feel differently about incest. I'm less able to say categorically or unequivocally that it's a bad thing. I'm more confused about the conditions under which it happens. I'm more cognizant of the trauma around incest. I'm not as able to say the perpetrator is terrible, awful, and that he should be locked up and the key thrown away. I think about the needs and wants of parents to get responses from their kids. I guess I'm more tolerant of deviant behaviors—not condoning, but more tolerant. I'm more perplexed now and less black and white in my opinions.

Peterson also felt he had changed: "The result of this situation is that I would react to incest or sexual abuse differently. I guess when you know the particulars in a case, you respond differently." Fincher admitted, "I've done a lot of reading about abuse and try to understand why people abuse. I guess I now have more empathy for 'abusers.'" Brookshire said: "I'm perhaps more tolerant of incest because I've seen the total picture in this case. I worry about whether it's really better for Darla if the father is penalized and the home is broken up." Roderick said:

> Darla's parents are really nice people. They seem like good parents. Jason might as well be where he is. I hope he's not institutionalized. Hudson County may shuffle it all under the rug—I suspect that is what will happen and it might be for the best. Even if the grandfather is the father, it might be best to leave him at home. I'm more tolerant because I know the family.

McNeil said, "Incest is culturally abhorrent and genetically unwise; still, I'm trying to get my feelings about this case sorted out." Tudor wondered: "In one way I would like to know if she's being abused at home now. But then, I feel it depends on who's being hurt or not being hurt."

UNDERSTANDING DARLA'S FAMILY

The literature suggests that professionals who provide services to children with special needs should attempt to be partners with the children's families (Peterson & Cooper, 1989; Seligman & Darling, 1989). Although many professionals originally were quite suspicious of members of Darla's family, most were able to move beyond their impressions to get a fuller understanding of the dynamics of the Helms' family life. There was a wide range of perceptions of the Helm family, and many admitted that their attitudes toward the family had fluctuated over time and they still had ambivalent feelings. Those who had more extensive contact with the family tended to be more positive than those with brief encounters. Among the Clay Center staff, Pam Brookshire had been at the Winthrop case conferences, at the trailer during Darla's maternity leave, and at Mapleton hospital.

> Darla's behavior shows that they have tried to train her. At home she does dishes and wipes counters. She knows what she's doing. Carol has high expectations and tends to treat Darla as higher functioning than she is. She talks to her all the time as if she understands. Missy, Darla's little sister, seems to enjoy Darla. She does not seem to be frightened of her, although Carol cautions her to "watch out" and "leave Darla alone." I did not observe Jimmy interact with Darla. They seem to avoid each other. The dad is the dominant type, but sometimes the mom does the talking, like the day they were at court for the sterilization hearing. Carol seemed upset. She kept saying, "Can you believe what is happening to my Darla?"

In Winthrop to relieve Carol about a week before Darla gave birth to Jason, Teresa Bellows observed:

> Carol, Dot, and Missy went shopping from 10 a.m. to 4 p.m. Darla knew me and was glad to see me. I brought puzzles and games and we worked on signing. It was clear that the family does not put demands on Darla. You could tell that she had not been working on signs. I kept her in the trailer. I was afraid of taking her on a walk. But Darla was restless, she paced. She jumped up and down and ran

around. There was a path worn in the carpet from Darla's room to the
kitchen, where Darla paced. Darla kept giving me hugs and she put
her feet in my lap for me to rub. She was uncomfortable and restless,
but she was in good humor. Carol was nice. She was grateful to get a
day out. It was obvious that she needed relief. There seemed to be no
embarrassment on the part of the family. Dot asked if Darla had
"gone after" me and seemed surprised that I wasn't upset that Darla
had pinched me. They were surprisingly calm and natural seeming, in
spite of having a daughter/granddaughter about to give birth.

Kelly Fincher provided respite care on three occasions: prior to Jason's birth,
at Southside Hospital, and in Winthrop after Darla and Jason were home from
the hospital. Fincher observed:

Dot was there. She was wild, strung out, and very active. She could
barely handle all of this. Carol was calm, but strained. She has a great
sense of humor and is very positive. The kids came home from school
while I was there. The kids and Carol are immaculate. They seem
intelligent, though not well-educated. Missy is adorable, funny, a
prankster, cute. She seemed very happy. She was loving with Dot and
Carol. She would try to interact with Darla. She watched what Darla
was doing, but she was reminded to keep away.
      At the hospital Dot and Carol were there. They had been there
since the baby was born on Monday and I went down on Wednesday.
Dot and Carol were both worn out. Dot went to sleep. They went out
for lunch together and stayed away for a couple of hours as I had encouraged them to do. I didn't observe any tension between them.
James called several times while I was there. He and Carol giggled on
the phone. Darla was active, she was up and down. Dot was hyper,
she was on Darla all the time. Carol was more laid back. She was
charting medicines. She didn't want Darla to have thorazine. She's a
tough lady. The doctor talked to me to try to get me to "convince
them she needs the medicine," but Carol has a real thing about medicines. You can't "convince" her of anything. Carol knows what she
wants for her daughter.

Three weeks after Jason's birth, Fincher observed:

It was clear that Missy loves the baby. Carol was more relaxed about
Missy interacting with Darla this time. Dot had gone home, even
though she was supposed to stay until Darla left for the Clay Center.
Nobody mentioned why she had gone. I wondered if she had

bothered them about the paternity. Nobody said anything. The family seemed to have come together to deal with the problems. I didn't observe any problems, except maybe with Jimmy.

Jimmy was observed briefly by Fincher on two occasions:

I saw Jimmy. He seemed older than 14. He was cute, adorable, quiet. He was just there. I don't remember any reaction—no emotion. Just quiet. After Jason was born, Jimmy came into the trailer toward the end of my visit. James and Jimmy came in together. James had an accident while they were working on their truck together. They came to get it taken care of. Jimmy seemed like a nice kid. He was kind of withdrawn about all this. Maybe he was worried about the suspicion about his father.

McCormick perceived Jimmy as a less prominent figure in the family even before Darla's pregnancy was discovered. In her weekly calls to Carol from the time Darla started at Clay, Jimmy was rarely mentioned. McCormick usually asked Carol about the children, and Carol would describe what Missy was doing, but never mentioned Jimmy. If asked specifically about him, Carol gave short, noninformative answers. McCormick evaluated: "It's almost as if he's a distant relative." A couple of weeks after Jason's birth, McCormick observed: "Jimmy was home from school. He was friendly to us. He offered us drinks when he was getting one for himself. He acted as if Darla was not there. He didn't really avoid her, but he didn't respond to her either. Darla acknowledged her parents—she might touch them, then she'd go pace back and forth. She didn't relate to Jimmy."

Many respondents spoke of patterns of parental dominance between the parents. McCormick noticed a switch in dominance after the pregnancy was revealed.

Mr. Helm seemed to be overprotective of Mrs. Helm. Then there was a definite change. Mr. Helm started to turn to Mrs. Helm for advice. Carol never had driven up to the Clay Center by herself. We got the feeling that he was trying to keep her from talking. She had seemed to be easily influenced by him, but after the pregnancy, she was more the one in charge.

A recreation assistant also noticed a change in roles: "There was a turn-around in Carol's behavior. At first James was assertive and Carol passive, then she started making decisions. She held up the fort emotionally."

Most individuals who had long-term contact with the Helm family felt that Carol was the more opinionated, assertive, and determined of the two parents. Jasper's impressions were unique.

> I got a picture of the family dynamics, of relations between Darla's mom and dad. I recognized that Mrs. Helm is less educated. The father is the decision maker. Carol is sort of like a teenaged girl talking to a boy when she talks to him. The grandmother, Dot, encourages this adolescent aspect of the relationship. Carol does not seem to make any decisions. She is manipulated by her mother and her husband. She was easily talked out of things, for example, the name of the baby. The grandmother is devoted to Darla. She relates remarkably well to Darla in terms of behavior management. She wants affection from Darla. However, she reads things into the relationship with Darla that aren't there. My problem is that she makes decisions for the family but then isn't there to live with the results of decisions.

Winthrop school personnel described Carol as the "one in charge," and James was generally described as playing a secondary supportive role in family dynamics. Community professionals had positive feelings about the family. Elise Yoder said:

> I admired Carol because she did a lot with Darla. Darla had a number of self-help skills. Carol was leery of the Clay Center because she worried about drugs and physical abuse. She was very careful. Carol also felt that sending Darla away meant that she had failed, but she recognized the need for help. As far as I could see, Carol and James agreed about Darla. I never observed any friction or dispute.

Yoder had known Jimmy since he was in primary school. At the time of Jason's birth, she was teaching at the high school, so she saw Jimmy, a first-year student, frequently in passing. Although they greeted each other, she had not had many conversations with him. She wanted to ask him about Darla, but didn't because she knew he had been embarrassed about her when he was younger and Yoder felt that she shouldn't mention Darla in front of other students. Yoder described Jimmy as a "quiet, nice, polite young man," and said: "He has only been paged to the office a couple of times, so you know he is not in much trouble. You hear many boys' names almost daily. He doesn't seem to be real interested in girls, at least not that you would notice, but he's pleasant and other kids seem to like him." Ken Ingalls had been impressed with the Helms' perseverance: "It's a functioning family." He later commented: "Maybe if the perpetrator is in the home, it's best if Darla is left there." Fred Quail sympathized: "I don't know. There's only so much people should be made to take."

Those in the medical community mainly reported positive feelings about family relations. Andrew Edge said: "That family can endure a lot. With other parents, Darla would have been institutionalized a long time ago. Carol even felt guilty about Darla going to the Clay Center. She worried about good care. She wrestled for months with the decision. She worried about quality time with her other children. Darla never had bruises. They never hit Darla." Yvonne Geneva said: "Carol is pushy—at times very pushy. But she has a goal. She's pushy because she is concerned about her family. She checks with us a lot about things. She gets us to help her make decisions, like about the sterilization and the C-section." Thomas Franklin categorized the family as "helpful" and "supportive." Jana Jones remarked: "I commend the mother for all she's done, unless, of course, she knew about the abuse and turned her head on something that she should have stopped." Carol was almost universally respected, although a number felt that they did not always understand her. Some believed that she might conceal the truth, particularly about family matters.

PROFESSIONAL EFFICACY

Not only were Clay Center and community professionals wary of how to respond to family members in the crisis of Darla's pregnancy, but many were suspicious of, and worried about, each other's roles related to caring for Darla. They were vociferous about their annoyance that certain doctors had refused to provide Darla with obstetrical care. Dr. Edge was disgusted at his colleague, Dr. Sheridan, and accused him of "worrying about himself, not Darla." Edge felt that Sheridan was afraid of legal ramifications and did not want to deal with a difficult patient. Carol Helm's criticism of Edward Sheridan was even more bitter: "He wanted nothing to do with Darla. He did not like her. He did not like me. I did not like him and Darla did not like him." Carol felt that not being able to do the sterilization was "just an excuse." When Carol told him about the tubal ligation, explaining that she herself had elected to have one a few years earlier, he informed her that "sterilization was wrong." He then refused to give her any names of other doctors who might be willing to have Darla as a patient. Carol's encounter with Sheridan and his refusal to treat Darla were traumatic for her. Dr. Franklin coincidentally practiced just down the hall from Dr. Sheridan in St. Teresa's Hospital. He, too, expressed annoyance at Sheridan for rejecting a patient such as Darla, and said the opposition to the sterilization was an excuse not to deal with a difficult patient and to avoid potential legal repercussions. It must be noted that about 15 other doctors also refused Darla as a patient, before Dr. Franklin consented to handle the case. At the same time, many admitted their own lack of preparedness and uneasiness in dealing with Darla's situation.

Around the time of Darla's pregnancy, there had been a series of news reports about the increasing number of Caesarean sections done in local hospitals. These reports had implied that doctors were doing them—and hospitals were allowing them—to earn more money delivering babies and to avoid potential lawsuits that might result from some flaw in the vaginal delivery of babies. Some interviewees thought there was wisdom in the selection of a Caesarean section for the delivery of Darla's baby; others were suspicious of professionals' motives. Respondents were divided about the types and amounts of medication given Darla and the use of restraints in the hospital.

Perhaps the greatest friction among professionals concerned the follow-up of the sexual abuse aspects of the case. Although this conflict played itself out in actual interactions between individuals, it also surfaced in informants' criticism of others during the interviews. To document this conflict, we digress to the sequence of events that occurred immediately after Darla's pregnancy was discovered.

Concern About Reported Abuse

After Clay Center staff returned from the family planning clinic on November 8 with the confirmation of Darla's pregnancy, they called Mark Johnson at State Protection and Advocacy to get advice on how to proceed. Mark had no concrete suggestions. At 3:10 p.m. Cindy McCormick contacted the welfare department in the Clay Center's home county. McCormick was disappointed when the local caseworker gave her a "so what" response to the news that a 15-year-old girl was pregnant. She was pleased that the attitude changed when the caseworker learned that Darla had autism. The welfare department social worker said that she would refer the case to Hudson County Child Protection in Darla's home county, where the abuse was likely to have occurred and where the investigation would take place.

Midmorning on November 9, McCormick again called the local welfare caseworker to report that the Helms had come to get Darla the night before. The caseworker assured McCormick that she had notified the Hudson County Welfare Department on the previous day. Clay staff assumed that they would be contacted by the Hudson County Welfare Department in the abuse investigation, but heard nothing in the next few days. When telephone calls to Carol Helm revealed that no investigation was taking place, Ken Ingalls was asked to call the Hudson County Welfare Department to check on what was being done.

On November 13, the Hudson County child protection worker, Donna Karnes, told Ingalls that she knew nothing about the case. She subsequently checked the papers on her desk and discovered the report from the Clay County Welfare Department. On November 14, Carol told McCormick that

Hudson Welfare had notified her that it had been reported that they [the Helms] had abused Darla. This was the first confirmation that an abuse investigation was being conducted. Abuse investigations are supposed to commence within 24 hours of the initial report. Almost a week had passed before this one started. A written report of investigation proceedings was to go to the reporting agency within 30 days; however, a report was not received by Clay Welfare until January 2, almost 2 months after the abuse was first reported. The report indicated that an abuse investigation had been initiated but was at a standstill until after the birth of Darla's baby, when blood tests could be done to determine paternity.

Clay employees, who felt extremely knowledgeable about Darla's case, were frustrated that they had never been contacted by Hudson County Child Protection workers. They worried that Hudson County agencies were not concerned with finding out who was responsible for Darla's pregnancy. Linda Morrow complained that the welfare department "took no visible action" until Jason was born. She was surprised that Donna Karnes never asked for information from Clay Center staff regarding Darla. Bellows said: "I was disappointed with Hudson County. I thought they were going to let it slide. We had to call them twice—once should have been enough. This is a punishable crime and the system should work like it's supposed to work."

Many members of the Clay staff attributed the local authorities' inaction to not caring about the case because Darla was retarded, and thus not "worth their trouble." According to Brad Parley:

> I was surprised by the whole attitude. I thought there would be more of a move to do something. The welfare department and everyone else where she's from were all a little too passive. I'm sure they would have done something in the case of a normal 15-year-old girl. This was pure taking advantage of a handicapped person. It was, after all, a clear-cut case of sexual abuse.

On November 21, a case conference was held in Winthrop to address the implementation of an educational program for Darla while she was pregnant. James and Carol Helm, Donna Karnes, Cindy McCormick, Linda Morrow, Margie Jasper, Ken Ingalls, and Fred Quail were present at that conference. Reflecting on her reactions to that meeting, Jasper explained:

> We were disappointed that caseworkers did not care to talk with us. We had information that we thought would be valuable for them in investigating the paternity aspect of the case. When we met Donna Karnes, we indicated our disappointment that more had not been done to determine who had sexually abused Darla. I was confrontive

in providing information, indicating that the nurses' examinations in-dicated continuing abuse rather than rape. The Helms said that per-haps Darla had used objects to penetrate her vagina in masturbation. (They had that argument ready!) The caseworker was surprised and asked about documentation from a doctor, saying that I was "just" a nurse and might not "really" know. I was concerned about alienating the family. I had prior experience with testifying against the parents of a teenaged girl. It was disruptive, painful. It tears a family apart. Darla does not fit the situation of a young child who might be removed from her home. She seems to have a loving family and no better living alternatives. Our fantasy was that the family would admit to the abuse happening and ask for counseling. But they denied it completely, which put us back. In the end our responsibility was to educate Darla and let other agencies handle their part.

At the February sterilization hearing, Clay staff again spoke up about the apparent "lack of commitment" to solving the case. Brookshire observed:

The judge was genuinely moved by the full day of testimony. He guaranteed that he would have the abuse investigated. We felt that, up until then, welfare had not done much. Apparently, they went to the house once, looked at it, talked to the parents, and that was it. Then the investigation stopped. Welfare could have tried harder to be an advocate for Darla.

McNeil said: "I couldn't figure out what the caseworker was doing. It wasn't clear that they had Darla's best interest in mind. The caseworker didn't want interference. I worried that there would be no legal retribution."

Dr. Franklin, who testified at the sterilization hearing, concurred with others' impressions about Clay staff's role: "Clay pushed for lab work. They made Donna Karnes consent to the blood tests to establish paternity." Although not present at the sterilization hearing, Ingalls and Quail verified Clay staff's assertive role at the first meeting in asking for information about proceedings regarding the abuse case and in pressuring child protection work-ers to take action. Both also accused the Hudson County Welfare Depart-ment of "being prone to do nothing" about such cases and noted that Karnes seemed to deny Clay staff's evidence and was defensive about her role. Ingalls provided an explanation for "Hudson County ways."

This is a conservative town where the family takes precedence. In this part of the state the family is held on a pedestal. I don't expect too much from welfare. At our Winthrop case conference for Darla in

November, Clay people kept bringing up the abuse. They gave information that was helpful. Welfare seemed not to be aware that the
sexual abuse had probably been a repeated thing and that it was probably a relative. Karnes thought Darla had probably been raped by an
outsider. Hudson County Welfare got a different look. They had their
eyes opened for them. The issue of probable incest was raised by Clay
staff. I've talked to Karnes three times on the phone about the case.
Somebody needed to pursue it to ascertain paternity and remove suspicion from others.

Quail claimed he had contacted the welfare department on three occasions about abuse cases among Winthrop students. Nevertheless, in spite of
having what Quail considered to be clear evidence, the welfare department
did "absolutely nothing." Quail resented the welfare department's manner
of handling those cases and stated the general opinion that the department
"did not pursue cases of abuse as hard as they could."

Karnes saw it differently. She claimed that Clay staff did not influence
the way she dealt with the case, although she was aware that Clay employees
were annoyed with her for "not performing miracles in solving the abuse case."
She insisted that they neither gave her new ideas about the situation nor
caused her to vary from her usual investigative techniques. In Karnes's opinion:

I proceeded in the only way possible in such a case. I interviewed all
the parties involved and tried to observe for hunches of who might be
responsible for abuse. I suggested that lie detector tests be given to all
possible perpetrators, but the prosecutor refused this method. Since
Darla could not reveal who had raped her, the blood tests were the
only means of getting evidence. Bettendorf and I consulted with
James and Carol and came up with the three males in the family who
had access to Darla: James Helm, Jimmy Helm, and Dale Helm,
Darla's uncle. All three men agreed to give blood samples, which
were scheduled for the time of Darla's delivery. Apparently, Clay personnel felt that Darla should be removed from the home, but I did
not have enough evidence for wardship. And I didn't think she was in
any life-threatening danger. I didn't think that removing her from her
home was the best thing for Darla. Even if the perpetrator is in the
home, she's best left there. We want the family to stay together as a
family. They've done well staying together so far. They got good supportive services from Clay. They don't need Mental Health right now.
It would just be more pressure on the family; another appointment to
keep—another stress.

Karnes had received three reports of sexual abuse regarding Darla: one from Clay personnel, one from the Clay County Welfare Department, and one from Dr. Sheridan. Karnes said she had not received a report from Andrew Edge, although she herself had initiated contact with him. Karnes knew that Clay staff were frustrated by "nobody doing anything about the abuse," but felt she had acted promptly—she had started the investigation on the day she received the report. She admitted that her actions soon came to a standstill because the victim, Darla, was nonverbal. Darla's case was a unique one for Karnes. She found her normal investigative methods inadequate. Karnes typically interviews the abused child, who usually names the perpetrator or describes the perpetrator if he or she is unknown to the victim. With Darla, Karnes was at a loss as to how to proceed.

Karnes asked for advice from local law enforcement officials, including the prosecuting attorney and the sheriff, and a mental health therapist, from whom she got "no ideas, only sympathy." Next, Karnes called the sexual abuse expert at the state-level welfare department in Capital City, a person she calls approximately four times a year for advice in difficult or unusual cases. Again, Karnes found no real help in the form of ideas on how to proceed, only support for the approach that she was taking. After consultation with the others, Karnes decided that the only way to gather evidence in this case was to wait 4 months for the baby to be born and then do blood tests. Karnes felt the investigation had to be "on hold" because of no new evidence.

In the meantime, she could provide support services to the family regarding medical bills and decisions involving Darla and the baby. Karnes said she visited the Helms' home on a few occasions and conducted individual interviews with each member of the family, including James, Carol, Jimmy, and Missy. Karnes evaluated the family as close knit and supportive. She felt they worked together as a unit. All members were cooperative and receptive to outside help. Karnes said that during the final months of Darla's pregnancy, Carol often used her as a "sounding board" before making decisions. Although Karnes described this case as "difficult" and "a challenge," she said that in many ways it was "just another case," and she was not overly concerned about it. In general, she described herself as "sensitive to people," saying that she "loves people" and that her heart went out to the Helms, thinking "poor child, poor family."

Karnes was confident that she was doing as much as she could to find the perpetrator of Darla's abuse. She felt that her years as a caseworker had led her to believe that, even in cases of abuse, the victim was often best left with the family. She knew that generally good foster-care facilities were hard to find, and that for a difficult child like Darla it was "almost impossible" to find a good placement. Karnes asserted that because of her awareness of these factors, her opinions about the Helms' situation were more realistic than those of others. She believed that this "informed perspective" was the result of long-term work in the field. She judged Clay staff to be "unrealistic and naive," but that "ignorance about sexual abuse investigation was common among the public." Karnes felt that "education of the public," including of lawyers and school officials, was a big part of her job. Although she admitted to being somewhat bothered by Clay staff's attitudes, Karnes "knew that their intentions were good; that they were mainly concerned with protecting Darla." She also believed that she had "gradually developed a good working relationship with Clay staff" and she expressed admiration and respect for the many Clay staff who volunteered to help the family before and after Jason was born, both in Winthrop and at Mapleton Hospital. Karnes felt their presence was a great support to the Helm family during a stressful time.

Donna Karnes had been in charge of child protection services for the Hudson County Welfare Department for a number of years. She met the Helms several years earlier when they contacted the welfare department for Crippled Children's Funds to help with a variety of expenses related to Darla's disability. Darla was Karnes's only client with autism, although she had seen programs on autism on television, so she felt that she knew something about the condition. She personally had no other clients with disabilities, but had considerable experience with teenage pregnancies. She estimated that she had investigated at least 10 cases of reported incest, although none of the victims had been pregnant. Karnes said that she handled at least one case of child abuse a month. Although she did not mention the school system, Karnes felt that she had a "good working relationship" with professionals from other Winthrop agencies (mental health, prosecutor's and sheriff's offices) who were involved in investigating cases such as this one. She stated that they were in "frequent communication" with each other.

Karnes's experience in the operating room during Darla's C-section was "a first" for her. Bettendorf had requested that she be present during the birth and blood-drawing to make sure the blood tests were properly done in case criminal charges were to be brought against the perpetrator. Karnes reported that this was the only sexual abuse case in which blood tests had been used in Hudson County. Because of the high level of reliability of the tests (99.94% accuracy), she predicted that they would be done more frequently in the future in cases of paternity dispute. Of course, suspects have to be willing to submit to blood tests; otherwise a search warrant is necessary and probable cause has to be established before a warrant is issued. Additionally, the blood tests are expensive and have to be paid for by the local welfare department.

Melvin Handly suggested several times that Paul Bettendorf should be interviewed. Carl Laidlaw and Fred Quail also recommended rather pointedly that the interviewer talk to Bettendorf. Bettendorf first agreed to be interviewed during a telephone conversation, then said that "evidence was coming in on sexual abuse" and that he would be "pushing ahead" with the case and was "not sure of what he could say." He agreed to be interviewed later in the summer when the case "settled down." A month later he refused to be interviewed because he said the case had "gone to juvenile court" and now was "all confidential" and he would not be able to talk about it at all. When told that Bettendorf had refused an interview on the grounds of confidentiality, Judge Handly said, "Oh, there's a lot he could say" and re-emphasized that Bettendorf should be interviewed.

Finally, 9 months after Jason's birth, when the case had been "more or less" settled, Bettendorf was contacted again. His silence on the other end of the line was countered with assurance that the interviewer had the Helms' permission. He agreed to respond to "nonconfidential" questions, adding: "This is a very unpleasant case. There has been a lot of emotion. Just because the Helms gave permission now does not mean they won't turn around and sue me later."

Mr. Bettendorf claimed not to have been taught anything about legal issues concerning people with disabilities in law school: "I was trained only to make sure that justice is done." According to Bettendorf, Darla is the only "autistic" in Hudson County. He could not remember having dealt with other people with disabilities either as perpetrators or victims of crime. He felt the experience of dealing with Darla was somewhat similar to dealing with abuse cases with very young children. In either case the victim is unable to understand or describe the crime. When the case goes to court, the victim cannot communicate with the jury. Bettendorf's main concern was getting "convictable evidence," and evidence was difficult to obtain if there were no witnesses and the victim was verbally limited. In Darla's case, pregnancy was evidence of a crime since she was under 16, and the blood tests might have produced "convictable evidence." However, because the perpetrator was a minor, the case went the Mental Health rather than the court route. Bettendorf claimed he "leaned on" the resources of Mental Health and Welfare when he felt that his information was inadequate, claiming "excellent" and "close" working relations, especially with Welfare. He had frequent contact with Donna Karnes, whom he called when he wanted to know something related to her clients.

As prosecutor, Paul Bettendorf is responsible for deciding whether to press charges in a case. Information about criminal acts comes to his attention through the sheriff's office, the state police, the welfare department, the Mental Health Clinic, or private individuals. When he receives information about a suspected crime, his decision about whether to prosecute is based on whether there is enough evidence to press charges. If there is not, he pursues it further himself, requests that other agencies investigate, or keeps in touch while others "do their work." In the Helm case he first was informed about the situation by Karnes, who had received various reports of child abuse regarding Darla. He decided not to "go with" lie detector tests because such evidence does not "hold up" in court. Subsequently he ordered Karnes to be present when Darla's baby was born and when the blood was drawn for the blood tests. He also got information from Karnes about her contact with family members and her home study. Often Bettendorf consults with Handly, Karnes, or others on how to pursue a case or ultimately when to press charges and take a case to court. He wants to make sure that he has enough evidence to convict a suspected party before he goes through the legal procedures. According to Bettendorf, in the Helm case, he "opted for the informal," that is, he let the case rest knowing that the family had agreed to counseling at the Mental Health Clinic. (It is important to note that since the case did not go to court, the counseling was not mandatory and the Helm family could choose to discontinue treatment at any time.) Bettendorf claimed to be "actively following the case."

Professionals as Adversaries

An important subplot in this story is the schism between Darla's needs for care and the community's resources for and manner of providing care. Darla's parents grew to see many professionals as adversaries rather than helpmates. When the Helms made accusations or were combative, professionals often became agitated and defensive themselves. This story illustrates that professionals must learn to recognize that intense parental reactions are natural, and often legitimate, responses to the extremely difficult situations they encounter as they attempt to meet their children's very unique needs. Carol and James had definitely learned the art of advocating for their child. On their own, they had sought out diagnoses, treatment, education, and residential services for their daughter whenever current services seemed inadequate. Unfortunately, in spite of the good intentions of many caring professionals, the Helms were thwarted and frustrated along the way.

Many of the professionals involved in Darla's case exhibited high levels of anxiety relative to their own security, and even their own competence, in performing their professional roles. In a climate of malpractice suits, many were suspicious about the potential risks to their professional futures if their behavior while caring for Darla was deemed unethical, illegal, or ill-advised. These threats may have loomed so large for some that they felt obligated to avoid Darla's situation altogether.

Carol Helm did not speak highly of doctors in general. She claimed that most she had dealt with were "uncaring, selfish, cold, and cruel." She made these statements emphatically and one could feel the force of emotion behind her words. When Carol found someone who would work conscientiously with Darla, she was extremely grateful. Carol found that person in Thomas Franklin and she worshipped him. Even Franklin was not perfect, however; he had

diagnosed Jason as microcephalic. But within a few months, after others confirmed this diagnosis, Franklin was forgiven.

Franklin was interviewed in his office shortly after 5:00 p.m. on a Friday
in June, just after he finished seeing his last patient. It was about 4 months
after Jason's birth. Franklin's hesitancy at the beginning of the interview indicated that, in spite of his belief that sterilization was a good choice for Darla,
he was still fearful about legal ramifications from the sterilization surgery he
had performed. Franklin felt that the information Clay staff presented in court
was realistic and convincing, and was presented in a professional manner. This
had eased his mind about the appropriateness of the sterilization decision.

In contrast to Franklin's willingness to be interviewed, several attempts
to reach Lowell Hanes, the obstetrician who had agreed to deliver the baby
if Darla went into labor prematurely, resulted in his receptionist's assurance
that the call would be returned. A couple of weeks after the interviewer's last
call to Hanes, suddenly she received a call at 10:30 on a Sunday night. Hanes
indicated that sterilization was "imperative" because of Darla's inability to care
for her contraceptive needs, and that a C-section, although not his own prefer-
ence, was an excellent choice for delivery of the baby because of Darla's
unique characteristics. After quickly making these statements, he concluded
the telephone call by saying, "I'll be glad to help. Let me know if I can help."
He hung up before the interviewer had the opportunity to ask any questions.

Dr. Edge and Yvonne Geneva, the nurse employed by Edge, were interviewed together. Geneva was clearly bothered that Edge said he had not been
in contact with social welfare or legal agencies in town; she promptly volunteered that he had talked to the "welfare people" and had "corresponded with
lawyers." Edge explained his hedging on this information by stating that there
were "many legal ramifications in the case." He nervously alluded to his having "given Darla some medication for upset stomach in the summer" and said
he would not have prescribed it if he had known that she was pregnant.

Darla's pregnancy presented a crisis for her family as well as for health
care providers, social service personnel, mental health clinicians, attorneys,
and educators. Decisions that would affect Darla's pregnancy, health, and
life-long protection required careful and thoughtful resolution. Darla's situation tested the limits of knowledge about autism, sexuality, and severe developmental disabilities. It forced a confrontation of attitudes about sexual
abuse and abusers, the rights of persons with developmental disabilities to
sexual fulfillment, abortion, sterilization, and parent advocacy. Embedded in
the subsequent days and months of deliberations were the common and con-
flicting views of those persons—parents and professionals—who struggled
to understand and make sense out of what had happened to Darla and what
Darla's pregnancy meant for her and for them.

CHAPTER 7

Epilogue

Jason was born on March 25; he and Darla went home on March 30. Six weeks later Darla returned to the Clay Center. At the end of May she went home for a weekend and then stayed at the Center until early September, when she spent a week at home. Darla continued to live at the Clay Center, with occasional weekends/weeks at home, throughout the subsequent year.

A YEAR, A MONTH, A WEEK, AND A DAY
AFTER JASON'S BIRTH

The final family interviews were conducted when Jason was 9 months old. Four months later, the person who did the family interviews got a message to call James Helm. When contacted, James stated that he did not want "the book" to end on a "sour note" and said that a number of things had happened since he was interviewed and that he had some "new information" to share. So, in early May, the interviewer spent a Sunday with the family at the trailer.

The difference in the family was astonishing: James was almost calm; Carol was bouncy, smiling, and outgoing. Jimmy seemed comfortable with his parents, and the accused, guilty look of previous months had almost vanished from his face. He mowed the large yard for about 2 hours, then, with a little frown, agreed to wash his father's car. Afterward, he convinced his dad to let him go for a drive before he had to be at work. Missy, who was recovering from chicken pox, chatted and joked with the interviewer. Then, in spite of her mother's prohibition, Missy slipped silently out the door to enjoy the warm spring day. Jason slept all morning, then "showed off for company"; when tired of that, he rather determinedly demanded his lunch. After eating he seemed content to play on a blanket for the next couple of hours.

James explained that at the time of his last interview he had been "very down," but since that time many of the family's problems had been somewhat resolved. James began: "You sometimes have to hit rock bottom before you can stand back and understand what is going on." Looking back, James believed that he was "at the point of being mentally ill." He was "literally torn up" about his family's situation. He claimed he "fought everyone" and was "particularly abusive with Carol," mostly mentally, but confessed that there was "physical abuse involved" of which he was "not proud." According to James, his marriage almost ended. James left home; he and Carol were apart for 3 or 4 days. James continued: "I was abusing the hell out of Jimmy and I didn't know it; mishandling every step. I was ranting and raving and blowing up over everything. I wanted to control everything and everybody and I couldn't. Everything kept getting worse."

While James was separated from his family, he thought things over and began to question the role he had been playing in the situation. James elaborated:

> I was egotistical and ignorant. I didn't think I could be wrong, but when I stood back and looked at myself I didn't like the way I'd been handling things. I was trying to look for answers, trying to right the wrong and see reason in the situation. But I was dealing with a situation that can't be handled. What I had to realize is that things happen without reason in this world—things just happen. I had to accept the fact that all was past and done—that I had to forget about everything and try to live the rest of my life right. I had to accept that there are some things that I can't accomplish—that can't be accomplished. That's been a life-long problem with me. I always think I should be able to accomplish more than I can. I try to take too much on; try to be a superman. With this whole thing, well, I can't solve it, I can't control it, so I might as well just put it out of my head.
>
> So, I've started out on a new track and found things not as bad as they once seemed. I've intentionally tried to put the family situation out of my head. It happened, but now I've got to put it behind me. You can't go on feeling a grudge or hate. You have to handle things with a laugh. It doesn't work to try to put things in place and keep them there. Anyhow, a lot of problems that used to tick me off now just seem too trivial—now I laugh. I enjoy solving problems now. You know, I never realized how easy it is to let go. When I did, I immediately felt better and I keep feeling better. Life has felt better since early April. I haven't felt this good since Darla was two. Life is easier to take.
>
> My change in behavior was a real relief for my family. We could get back together again. I cannot forget what happened, but I can forgive Jimmy. He still suffers—he always will. But I'm his father. I've got to help him lead a normal life. With the load he has to carry he'll need my help. I don't want him to be held back because of something

he did when he was 14 years old. I want to take care of my family. My role as a parent is to help my son.

During the 2 months since the reconciliation, father and son had spent time with each other. James taught Jimmy to drive and helped him get his driver's license. They fixed up their old car for Jimmy to use. James seemed pleased that Jimmy had a girlfriend, and he explained that they have started to let Jimmy date. James said they have allowed "controlled dating," which meant that Jimmy and Stephanie were allowed three dates a month. Otherwise they could see each other at school or talk on the phone. Stephanie's parents were divorced and her father had custody of her; however, she had been raised mainly by family friends, Scott and Tammy. The Helms have had several get-togethers with Scott, Tammy, and Stephanie. The previous week, Scott and Tammy organized a hayride in which about 40 people took part. According to both James and Carol, they "had a ball." The families also had a couple of cook-outs together, and sometimes they just spent the evening talking.

One problem with the family friendship was that it interfered with the "controlled dating." James said that while the adults socialized, the teenagers had too much opportunity to "put their arms around each other." He and Carol had been puzzled about how to deal with this. First they told Jimmy that family occasions counted as dates. The Helms had invited Stephanie's family for a barbecue on the evening of the interviewer's visit. After talking on the telephone with Stephanie, Jimmy announced that she would not be coming to dinner with Scott and Tammy because they preferred to "use" their allotted "date" to go to a movie on Friday. James winked and said, "Tell Stephanie to come and I won't count it as a date." James projected that after about 6 months of controlled dating they will allow Jimmy more freedom for "real dating."

James and Carol both liked Stephanie and felt that she was good for Jimmy. She was 17 and a year ahead of Jimmy in school. James pointed out that she was the oldest child in a split home and had been forced to shoulder a lot of responsibility. She was still upset about family problems. James felt that because of similarities in Stephanie's and Jimmy's situations, they could help each other. He conjectured that teenagers could help each other work out problems better than an adult could.

The Helms were pleased that Jimmy continued to do well at school and that he was responsible about his work at the restaurant. He was working about 12 hours a week, and although he would prefer more hours, he had saved about $400 in 4 months. Carol jokingly, but proudly, called Jimmy a "tightwad," saying he was reluctant to spend his money. She added that he did spend it on Stephanie. Carol teased Jimmy about his reaction to an occasion at McDonald's when she pretended to have no money and asked Jimmy to treat her. Apparently Jimmy was quite bothered at having to dip into his own pocket. Carol chided Jimmy that he would spend money on Stephanie, but not on her. Jimmy frowned and said, "But you guys have your own money. You have more money than me."

Jimmy was no longer seeing Hugh, the psychologist, but had been assured that he could call if he needed help. Hugh periodically called to find out how things were going. Actually, in the end, it was mainly James who was seeing Hugh. According to James, "My problems were greater than anybody's. I was so low that it was either give up or really try to make a comeback. I looked in the mirror and got nothing back. I needed the help." The switch to Hugh from the first counselor, Nancy, had come easily. Nancy was cutting her caseload and so they were transferred to Hugh. James had wanted a male counselor for Jimmy so this worked fine. When asked if they thought having a male made a difference, James said "yes," but Carol interjected that it wasn't the maleness or femaleness that counted but rather the fact that the two counselors had different styles, and she thought that Hugh's was more effective with their family. Nancy mainly listened; there is "more input" from Hugh. According to James, "Hugh says what he thinks. He confronts our remarks." For example, Hugh might say, "You're being narrow-minded, aren't you?" Carol called Hugh "a pleasant person who is comfortable to be with," "a card," and "not as serious as Nancy." James hypothesized that it might be their training and status that made a difference: Hugh was a "psychologist" and Nancy "only a counselor." James added that neither was a "psychiatrist" or "psychoanalyst." In retrospect, James recalled that he did not like Hugh at first, but now realized that Hugh was "right" and he was "wrong." In the end, James readily admitted that he needed help and appreciated the mental health counseling.

Perhaps one of the biggest changes for the Helms was that they now had a family-oriented social life. Carol beamed as she related:

> We've met people and they like us! We've gotten to the point that we almost have too many friends—more than we can handle. At first it was hard knowing how to deal with friends—we'd never had any when Darla was home. Now when people drop in at first I think, "Now why are they here again?" But that's what friends do. With Darla here we had to stay home, and even when friends came over we weren't able to really enjoy them because Darla would do something weird and everybody would be nervous. Now we are flexible. We can accept invitations to barbecues and hayrides. It's great!

Carol had changed dramatically in 6 months. She smiled continually, smoked less, and was not stiff with shoulder pains. Looking back, she believed that the pain was largely the result of tension and stress. Carol attended aerobic classes three mornings a week with two friends. The spa had a sitter service where she could leave Jason. One of her friends had a 4-month-old daughter and they often went shopping together or out for a cup of coffee after they exercised. Carol clearly enjoyed the social contact.

Another important occurrence was that the Helms had made an offer on a house. They both loved the house and were anxiously optimistic about securing the financing they needed. (They moved into the house a few months later.) The house was 2 miles north of the courthouse, very close to Winthrop High School. Carol confided that the neighborhood was a "little snobbish," but when asked if she worried whether they would fit in and be accepted, she confidently said, "They'll like us." The house has a large wooded lot that is nicely landscaped. It has four, potentially five, bedrooms. One bedroom on the ground floor has no windows, and although the rest of the house is wallpapered or painted in light colors, this room has sturdy wood paneling. As they were being shown the house, the present owners apologized for the windowless room, but James and Carol turned to each other and laughed. Both had already recognized this as the perfect room for Darla, who tended to smudge walls and peel wallpaper and could not be trusted around windows. Additionally, the room was located next to the ground-level family room, with a durable carpet over a cement floor. Carol remarked, "Darla can jump to her heart's content and not go through the floor." They had already fallen in love with the house, but "being right for Darla" convinced them that it was "their house." Carol had been looking at houses for 6 weeks and had seen some "wonderful houses" and "good deals," but none of them were right for Darla. They would not have been safe for her. She would have "destroyed them in a day."

Even though they kept Darla in mind as they searched for a house, neither James nor Carol expected Darla to return to being a permanent, full-time member of the household. Carol says:

> During all those early years I gradually got used to taking care of Darla 24 hours a day. Caring for Darla was my life. It was normal then. I was not even aware of her impact on the rest of the family—of what we were sacrificing. But now that she has been at the Clay Center for 2 years, I've established a life of my own and I don't think that I could survive with Darla here full time. I can't go back to that.

James turned to the interviewer and added, "You've spent a peaceful day in our home: Jimmy working, Missy playing, Jason being good. If Darla had been here we would not have had 10 minutes to talk. There would have been no peace. We would have to watch her constantly and we would all be distracted. Things go haywire when she's here."

Carol believed that she was becoming more able to "let go" of Darla. She found herself not always thinking about Darla. Carol maintained that she loved Darla, but was not as wrapped up in her as she had been 2 years ago. Carol stated:

Darla knows who I am. She does love me, but I really don't think that she cares that much. Basically, she doesn't need us. She gets bored with us. She is alright for a while and then she starts expecting things. She seems to want a change. Darla would have to change tremendously before I'd take her back. She would have to mellow out. Maybe she will someday, perhaps after she's an adult.

James added, "But in the meantime, we can't do anything with her—anything for her. We have taken Darla as far as our knowledge can take us. Here she can't make progress. We need experts. But it still makes me uncomfortable to have my family spread across the country."

When asked whether they would choose to be parents if they could do it over again, both Carol and James laughed, hesitated, and almost simultaneously responded, "Not if we knew we'd have a child like Darla." Carol continued, "No one in his right mind would ask to have a retarded child, especially an autistic child. Of course I say that now—I say one thing and do another. We did not have to take Jason. We knew he would probably be retarded, but we took him." James interrupted, "Yes, we did have to take him. Jason is our grandson. We had to take him. But Jason is different than Darla. He's got the darndest personality. He is constantly loveable. He's easy-going and affectionate. He loves to be hugged and kissed and talked to."

At 13 months Jason seemed more like a 5- to 7-month-old baby. He scooted his walker backward, but it seemed more like an accidental motion than a deliberate one. Carol claimed that he "crawls like an inchworm," but he stayed in one place for a couple of hours during the interview, apparently watching the sunlight, glancing at the television, and occasionally rolling from his back to his stomach. According to James he loves the grill on the air-conditioner and would run his hands across it to make a rattling sound. He plays with rattles and squeaky toys. In general, he likes noises, and babbles loudly and makes a variety of sounds when he is off by himself. James said that once he watched/listened to a violin concert on television for about 2 hours. When he is held by his family or by outsiders he stares and seems to be interested in faces. He smiles in response to talk, smiles, or laughter. Carol said that he likes to grab onto teeth and once he pulled a visitor's false teeth out of her mouth.

Jason seemed to sleep more than most children his age; his morning nap lasted at least 3 hours. When he woke up he did not cry or yell for attention.

He did indicate when he was hungry by yelling in a deep, loud, pulsating tone. He stopped yelling immediately when Carol talked to him and didn't yell when she was making food preparation noises. When she stopped to talk to the adults, Jason promptly began to yell again.

James and Carol admitted that Jason's development was slow; they also pointed out that he had progressed steadily. His eyes no longer jerked back and forth as rapidly or as constantly and it was clear that he was focusing on things up to a distance of at least 6 feet. It was also apparent that he could recognize his favorite toys and objects, and knew the members of his family. He watched Carol particularly and seemed to be calmed and reassured by interaction with her. To outsiders Jason's head was noticeably small, but James and Carol amusedly asserted that he looked "normal" to them. Carol was the godmother of 4-month-old Shannon, who was very chubby and had a large, round head. Carol laughed as she described an incident in McDonald's. Carol was left to care for the two babies while her friend went to the restroom. A nosey waitress asked Carol if Shannon was "mongoloid or something, because her head was so big." The waitress did not remark on the smallness of Jason's head, but praised his pretty blue eyes.

It was heartening to see that James and Carol are more sure of their role regarding Jason; Carol is "Mom" and James is "Pa." They both appeared to genuinely love the child and enjoy taking care of him. It was also good to see Jimmy acting like a typical teenager, although he seemed to be better-behaved and more respectful of his parents than most. He was very much included in their thoughts and lives. Missy was outgoing and cheerful. She was affectionate with her parents and Jason. Although the Helms discussed problems and were worried about Darla's future, they were determined to have more fun on a day-to-day basis and were not willing to let concern for her or their other problems dominate their lives.

NOBODY'S RESPONSIBILITY

In spite of acknowledging that they did not feel able to have Darla at home on a full-time basis, the Helms did not have definite plans for Darla's future. Unfortunately, Darla had made little progress at the Clay Center; in fact she had regressed in some ways. Staff found that she frequently was very difficult to manage; it took one full-time person to keep track of her and prevent her from injuring herself or others. The other clients were able to take part in community integration activities, but often Darla's behavior kept her from the programming she needed. As a result, at the March case review, it had been made clear to the Helms that the soon-to-be-17-year-old Darla would have to leave the Clay Center at the end of June.

   The Helms had been informed of the likelihood of Darla's termination and had expected it, but still were bothered that the placement had not worked out. James commended Clay staff for being "extremely good" with Darla and for being "the only people they trusted." They were used to having Darla at the Clay Center and, although it was more than 100 miles from their home, they thought that it was likely to be closer than any subsequent placement. Carol and James argued that Darla had made progress, even though it might not be apparent to Clay staff. James acknowledged that Darla had always fought structure and was obstinate enough to recognize what people wanted her to do, and do the opposite. She always related to direct instruction in this manner. When pressure is put on her to perform a task or behave in a certain way, she "blows up." He said that he could empathize with staff's frustrations but believed that they were "giving up too soon."

   In addition to the disappointment that Darla would not be permitted to continue at the Clay Center, James was annoyed that people at the last conference did not "respect his intelligence." He pointed out that parents of children with autism are knowledgeable about their children and are fully aware that they are difficult to manage. He maintained that having a child with autism makes you realistic. He said that parents understand management problems—in fact, the whole situation—and know that agencies have a business to run. He said that he wished that staff would respect his perceptions and his intelligence and deal with him in an honest, direct, and open manner. James and Carol excitedly pointed out that people had given them "little excuses" for "giving up on Darla." When questioned about their meaning, James clarified that people kept mentioning that the doctor associated with Clay Center felt he could not treat Darla appropriately and that he would be "liable" if Darla injured herself or harmed others. The Helms maintained that the only way a doctor could be liable is if the doctor "did something to her." They had signed many papers that released professionals from liability for anything. Carol was "pissed" that people felt that they had to "come up with silly things like that." After letting off steam about that occasion, they proceeded to praise the expertise and caring manner of professionals at the Clay Center.

   James contended:

> As far as making plans for the future, we can only take things one day at a time. The only thing that I know is that I could never let Darla go to a state hospital. She could really get messed up. I don't trust institutions. Sure, they put on a show for visitation, clean up their act, but the next day when no one's watching it's totally different. Darla is still trainable. We want her to stay in a training program and not go some place where she'll sit all day. We'll pressure the local school system until they find a training program.

During the year that Darla turned 17, Clay Center staff and Winthrop school personnel met several times with the Helms concerning future placement for Darla. The State Department of Education, the State Department of Mental Health, and the Winthrop School Corporation had the responsibility of finding a suitable program by the end of that fiscal year. Since an appropriate program was not found, the Clay Center agreed to keep Darla for one more year under a special contract that supported a totally individualized program for her. That agreement, which was signed by the state agencies and the parents, stipulated that Darla's program would be carefully documented so that the next placement, which was to start on or before June 30, would be equipped to plan for her adult years.

Clay staff were avidly involved in documenting information about Darla that could be transferred to another placement. They felt that a long-term plan needed to be put into effect for her as early as possible. Over the course of the year, Darla gained new recreational and vocational skills, but she still required constant supervision, a protective environment, and a highly structured program. The staff felt that she would not yet be ready for the type of group homes that were available.

Planning for the transition started in November, but it was not until spring that Department of Mental Health personnel identified a possible placement for Darla. In April, Clay staff met with the State Developmental Center (SDC) staff and the Helms to examine the recommended facilities. Clay staff felt that the SDC personnel were knowledgeable and would be receptive to being trained to provide an appropriate training program for Darla, and a plan for a smooth transition was arranged. However, on closer inspection, both Clay staff and the Helms found the living conditions on the unit to be unacceptable. The Helms asked the SDC administration to provide a Medicaid-certified unit since Darla is eligible for Medicaid. This request was refused, so, with no place for Darla to live, the training arrangement had to be rejected. The Helms wrote letters explaining why the program was unacceptable and continued to insist on something appropriate for their daughter.

Ken Ingalls was also actively seeking alternative placements. He suggested the possibility of an intermediate care facility for people with mental retardation, with an in-home teaching arrangement. The local Case Manager for Mental Health said that respite money could be made available for this arrangement. Someone from the Department of Education informed Clay Center staff that in-home program arrangements had been worked out and would be offered to the Helms for consideration. Carol and James again rejected the offer. They reasoned that it was a short-term solution for Darla and they did not want to settle for that. It became apparent that interagency agreements were difficult to operationalize.

Notified that Darla would have to leave the Clay Center on June 30, Carol and James filed for a hearing on Friday, June 26. Letters were received by agencies on the following Monday and Tuesday, June 29 and 30. At some point, Carol and James called the State Protection and Advocacy Agency and were advised that Darla had the right to remain in her current placement until an alternative placement was found. It was promptly clarified that this advice was based on the state law applying to local school settings, but was not relevant to Clay programming. Meanwhile, the Clay Center was placed in a precarious and very stressful position: Their special contract was ending that day, the trained staff were fulfilling their last obligations before leaving, and there was no safe and appropriate place for Darla. Some of the Clay staff agreed to remain for a few hours in a respite capacity, and such a plan went into effect at midnight on the day the contract ended.

On Wednesday morning, July 1, legal counsel was sought by Clay Center administrators. From that point on, attorneys, judges, case managers, educators, administrators, doctors, and others were consulted. The general consensus was that since the Clay Center had custody, no one else would take responsibility. The contract had ended, and Clay Center personnel had to act. Everyone at the Clay Center was concerned about Darla and her safety. Because of the forthcoming long holiday weekend, time was running out. After many telephone calls, possible respite sources were located, but Darla could change locations and programming only with the authority of the Clay Center's local county court and Winthrop's county court. In the end it turned out that the only legal course of action was to deliver Darla to her parents. A few weeks earlier, Carol and James had gone to court to secure legal guardianship, since Darla had turned 18 and was therefore an emancipated adult. Because of the guardianship, Darla could become the court's responsibility only if the parents were found to be negligent in their parenting responsibilities. Negligence, in this case, would be their refusal to receive their daughter when she was returned home or their absence from home if they had been informed about the approximate time of arrival.

On Thursday, July 2, the Clay Center attorney called James and told him that the staff would be bringing Darla home that afternoon, and the attorney provided an approximate time of arrival. James protested that Darla needed an appropriate placement. The attorney responded that such an issue was between the parents, the State Department of Education, and the local schools. So, as promised, later that day four Clay Center staff, accompanied by the Center attorney, drove Darla home. In the van, Darla ate the supper that had been packed for her by Clay Center staff. One stop was made for Darla to use a restroom. Darla was a cooperative passenger—calm and quiet during the trip. They arrived in Winthrop at 6:30 p.m. and delivered Darla and her belongings, including medications, to her parents. Darla bounced out of the van and hugged her mother. Carol and James received Darla affectionately. They apologized to Clay Center staff for the staff's having to transport their daughter from the Center to their home, but said that they could not give consent to a change in placement until an appropriate placement had been found. They felt that if they had transported Darla home themselves, it would have constituted consent. Clay staff and the attorney were relieved to witness Darla's welcome by her parents.

CONCLUSION

Why has pregnancy been reported so rarely among those with autism? Part of the answer may be due to the characteristics of people with autism. By definition, they have limited abilities to communicate and to form normal social relationships. They typically respond poorly to new situations or people, and they often show strange, erratic, and aggressive behaviors that make others leery of approaching them. Thus, they are not likely to be attracted to others, to know how to approach others, or to be sufficiently passive to approaches from others for sexual relations to occur. These conditions would seem to be exacerbated in cases where there is also severe mental retardation.

There were also situational factors that could explain the lack of documented reproduction among this population. In the past, it was common for individuals with mental retardation—and autism—to be sterilized when they reached puberty, or to be confined to institutions that practiced segregation of the sexes and offered little privacy to residents. Their situations were deliberately structured to prevent pregnancies. Lastly, families and communities may have kept stories, such as Darla's, secret. If Darla's pregnancy had been identified earlier, and an abortion had been carried out, there would have been few consequences for Darla or her family. Had the family waited another few months before requesting the residential placement, they would have discovered the pregnancy (and probably the cause) quietly themselves.

It is necessary to develop an understanding not just of autism as a condition, not just of individuals with disabilities, not just of family strengths and weaknesses, but of the whole community's responsibility for caring for people in a flexible and resilient way that allows dignity and still provides support. Perhaps to do this, each of us must first acknowledge the ways in which our own limited experiences and prejudices may blind us to realities that do not fit our accepted assumptions. Perhaps Darla's story can shock us into beginning such a quest.

The 1990 American Disabilities Act (PL101-336) made it illegal to discriminate against individuals with disabilities in employment, public accommodations, public services, and telecommunications (Paul, Porter, & Falk, 1993). Yet, in Darla's case, appropriate treatment was hard to find. If certain individuals had not come to their rescue, Darla's family could easily have failed to find tolerable care for her during her pregnancy. Darla's story presents a less than totally positive commentary on the tendency of the state's legal and educational systems to be at odds with family wishes and client needs, and to function at cross-purposes with each other. It demonstrates the gaps in planning as professionals and families attempt to communicate, collaborate, and provide for the protection, care, and education of people with disabilities. Individuals such as Darla require a strong and extensive commitment from agencies to work cooperatively.

Information about Darla and her situation was learned by many people over the course of 3 years. The story, sadly, forces the realization that supportive legal, medical, social welfare, mental health, residential, and educational systems so desperately needed by people like Darla, are just not in place. Our hope is that the information transmitted in this story will facilitate understanding and awareness, so that progress toward humane and appropriate services can occur. Jason, like his mother, will need protection, care, and education. We hope his story will be different.

APPENDIX A

People Who Figure
in Darla's Story

The following list included some people (marked °) who were observed but not interviewed and others (marked †) who were neither observed nor interviewed, but were referred to in interviews with others.

Helm Family

°Darla Helm, 15-year-old with autism and mental retardation
Carol Helm, Darla's 33-year-old mother
James Helm, Darla's 34-year-old father
°Jimmy Helm, Darla's 14-year-old brother
°Missy Helm, Darla's 5-year-old sister
°Jason, Darla's infant son
°Dot, Carol's 48-year-old mother
†Mr. & Mrs. James Helm, James's parents
°Dale Helm, James's younger brother
†Denise Helm Bettendorf, James's younger sister
°Sharon, a friend of the Helm family

State Officials

Mark Johnson, Lawyer at Protection and Advocacy
Arno Green, Lawyer at Protection and Advocacy
Linda Paskin, Lawyer at Protection and Advocacy
Susan Andrews, Department of Education, Consultant for Emotional Handicaps

Winthrop/Hudson County Professionals

Donna Karnes, Hudson County Child Protection Worker
Melvin Handly, Hudson County Court Judge

Paul Bettendorf, Winthrop Prosecuting Attorney
Carl Laidlaw, Helm Family Lawyer
Richard Vaughn, Winthrop Lawyer, Guardian ad Litem
Fred Quail, Superintendent, Winthrop Schools
Ken Ingalls, Special Education Director, Winthrop Schools
†Rita Burton, First Teacher, Moderate Class
†Janey Tellingho, Second Teacher, Moderate Class
Elise Yoder, Third Teacher, Moderate Class
†Anthony Wilder, Winthrop Pediatrician
Andrew Edge, Winthrop Family Practitioner
Yvonne Geneva, Nurse in Edge's Practice
†Nancy, Mental Health Counselor
†Hugh, Mental Health Psychologist

Mapleton Medical Personnel

†Edward Sheridan, OB/GYN at St. Teresa's Hospital
Thomas Franklin, OB/GYN at St. Teresa's Hospital
Jana Jones, Obstetrical Nurse at Southside Hospital
†Victor Shelby, Pediatrician present at Jason's Birth
†Paul Lovell, Resident Psychiatrist, Mapleton Clinic
†Martin Lynton, Director of East Coast Clinic

Clay Center Staff

Chuck Giesler, Director, Clay Center
Sandra Werner, Associate Director, Clay Center
Linda Morrow, Coordinator, Autism Program
Cindy McCormick, Social Worker
Margie Jasper, Nurse
Kelly Fincher, Home Programmer
Pam Brookshire, Recreation Therapist
Felicia Tudor, Creative Arts Instructor
Jerry Roderick, Speech Therapist
Bill Peterson, Teacher
Teresa Bellows, Classroom Aide
Brad Parley, Classroom Aide
Nurhan Tokar, Residential Night Supervisor
Lisa McNeil, Residential Day Supervisor
Bob Birmingham, University/Clay Center Lawyer
(Sixteen other Clay Center staff members were interviewed, but because
of the limited extent they were quoted, they will remain unnamed.)

Clay City/County Professionals

Fran Ellis, Nurse Practitioner at Family Planning Clinic
Lowell Hanes, OB/GYN

Medical Center (in State Capital) Employees

Shelley Hunt, Pediatrician, Director of Newborn Clinic
†Art Kincady, Geneticist, Newborn Clinic

APPENDIX B

Interview Protocol

1. How long have you known Darla and/or her family and what is the nature of your interaction? (When did you first meet them? How often do you see them now? How has your relationship with them changed over time?)

2. What are your impressions of Darla? (What does she look like? Describe her behavior when you have been with her. Has she changed during the time you've known her?)

3. Do you know others who are similar to Darla? (Who? What was the context of your acquaintance?)

4. What experiences have you had with children or adults with disabilities?

5. What experiences have you had with pregnancy of adolescents?

6. What was your reaction to learning of Darla's pregnancy?

7. How do you feel about the decisions that were made concerning Darla's pregnancy and delivery?

8. How did you feel about the sterilization? (How do you feel about sterilization for others? for people who are retarded?)

9. What is your sense of Darla's understanding of sexual intercourse? pregnancy? childbirth? rearing a child?

10. What was your responsibility for (role regarding, interaction with) Darla during, and/or subsequent to, her pregnancy? Did you have any concerns about your role? What were those concerns?

11. What are your impressions of/feelings about Darla's family? mother? father? brother? sister? baby?

12. What is your perception of the relationships among family members?

13. What are your impressions of their reactions to the situations surrounding the pregnancy?

14. What type of contact have you had with Clay Center staff? What are your impressions of Clay Center services? What is your sense of relations between Clay Center staff and Darla's family? professionals outside the Clay Center?

15. What type of contact did you have with other agencies and individuals about this case? What are your impressions of their involvement?

References

Alaszewski, A., & Ong, B. N. (Eds.). (1990). *Normalisation in practice*. London: Tavistock/Routledge.

Beauchamp, T. L., & Childress, J. F. (1989). *Principles of biomedical ethics* (3rd ed.). New York: Oxford University Press.

Bogdan, R., & Taylor, S. J. (1982). *Inside out: The social meaning of mental retardation*. Toronto: University of Toronto Press.

Brantlinger, E. A. (1983). Measuring variation and change in attitudes of residential care staff toward the sexuality of mentally retarded persons. *Mental Retardation, 21*, 17–22.

Brantlinger, E. A. (1988a). Teachers' perceptions of the parenting abilities of their secondary students with mild mental retardation. *Remedial Education and Special Education, 9*, 31–43.

Brantlinger, E. A. (1988b). Teachers' perceptions of the sexuality of their secondary students with mild mental retardation. *Education and Training in Mental Retardation, 23*, 24–37.

Brantlinger, E. A. (1991a). Home–school partnerships that benefit children with special needs. *The Elementary School Journal, 91*, 249–260.

Brantlinger, E. A. (1991b). The influence of teacher gender on students' access to knowledge about their sexual and intimate social selves. *Feminist Teacher, 5*, 25–29.

Brantlinger, E. A. (1992a). Sexuality education in the secondary special education curriculum: Teachers' perceptions and concerns. *Teacher Education and Special Education, 15*, 32–40.

Brantlinger, E. A. (1992b). Professionals' attitudes toward the sterilization of people with disabilities. *Journal for the Association for Persons with Severe Handicaps, 17*, 4–18.

Burgdorf, R. L., Jr. (1983). Freedom of choice: Competency and guardianship. In R. L. Burgdorf, Jr., & P. P. Spicer (Eds.), *The legal rights of handicapped persons: Cases, materials, and text* (pp. 209–222). Baltimore: Paul H. Brookes.

Diamond, S. (1993). Growing up with parents of a child with a disability: An individual account. In J. L. Paul & R. J. Simeonsson (Eds.), *Children with special needs: Family, culture, and society* (pp. 53–77). Fort Worth, TX: Harcourt Brace Jovanovich.

Edgerton, R. B. (1967). *The cloak of competence*. Berkeley: University of California Press.

Featherstone, H. (1981). *A difference in the family.* New York: Penguin.

Geertz, C. (1973). *The interpretation of cultures.* New York: Basic Books.

Glaser, B., & Strauss, A. (1965). *Awareness of dying: A study of social interaction.* Chicago: Aldine.

Glaser, B., & Strauss, A. (1967). *The discovery of grounded theory: Strategies for qualitative research.* Chicago: Aldine.

Gleason, J. J. (1989). *Special education in context: An ethnographic study of persons with developmental disabilities.* Cambridge: Cambridge University Press.

Greenfield, J. (1965). *A child called Noah.* New York: Holt, Rinehart and Winston.

Greenfield, J. (1978). *A place for Noah.* New York: Holt, Rinehart and Winston.

Harris, J. (1990). Wrongful birth. In D. R. Bromham, M. E. Dalton, & J. C. Jackson (Eds.), *Philosophical ethics in reproductive medicine* (pp. 156–170). Manchester: Manchester University Press.

Henshel, A-M. (1972). *The forgotten ones: A sociological study of Anglo and Chicano retardates.* Austin: University of Texas Press.

Hunt, N. (1967). *The world of Nigel Hunt: The diary of a mongoloid youth.* Beaconsfield, England: Finlayson.

Jackson, J. C. (1990). Withholding neonatal care 2. A philosopher's view. In D. R. Bromham, M. E. Dalton, & J. C. Jackson (Eds.), *Philosophical ethics in reproductive medicine* (pp. 124–139). Manchester: Manchester University Press.

Janko, S. (1992). Beyond harm: A case study of the social construction of child abuse. In P. M. Ferguson, D. L. Ferguson, & S. J. Taylor (Eds.), *Interpreting disability: A qualitative reader* (pp. 38–60). New York: Teachers College Press.

Lilford, R. (1990). What is informed consent? In D. R. Bromham, M. E. Dalton, & J. C. Jackson (Eds.), *Philosophical ethics in reproductive medicine* (pp. 211–261). Manchester: University of Manchester Press.

Mattinson, J. J. (1971). *Marriage and mental handicap.* Pittsburgh: University of Pittsburgh Press.

Paul, J. L., Beckman, P., & Smith, R. L. (1993). Parent and sibling perspectives. In J. L. Paul & R. J. Simeonsson (Eds.), *Children with special needs: Family, culture, and society* (pp. 77–96). Fort Worth, TX: Harcourt Brace Jovanovich.

Paul, J. L., Porter, P. B., & Falk, G. D. (1993). Families of children with disabling conditions. In J. L. Paul & R. J. Simeonsson (Eds.), *Children with special needs: Family, culture, and society* (pp. 3–24). Fort Worth, TX: Harcourt Brace Jovanovich.

Perske, R., & Perske, M. (1988). *Circle of friends: People with disabilities and their friends enrich the lives of one another.* Nashville, TN: Abington Press.

Peterson, N. L., & Cooper, C. S. (1989). Parent education and involvement in early intervention programs for handicapped children: A different perspective on parent needs and the parent-professional relationship. In M. J. Fine (Ed.), *Second handbook on parent education: Contemporary perspectives* (pp. 197–252). San Diego, CA: Academic Press.

Ruble, L. A., & Dalrymple, N. J. (1993). Social/sexual awareness of persons with autism: A parental perspective. *Archives of Sexual Behavior, 22*(3), 229–240.

Schwier, K. M. (1990). *Speakeasy: People with mental handicaps talk about their lives in institutions and in the community.* Austin, TX: ProEd.

Seligman, M., & Darling, R. B. (1989). *Ordinary families, special children: A systems approach to childhood disability.* New York: Guilford.

Sloan, I. J. (1988). *The law governing abortion, contraception, and sterilization.* London: Oceana Publications.

Stepan, N. L. (1991). *"The hour of eugenics": Race, gender, and nation in Latin America.* Ithaca, NY: Cornell University Press.

Stump v. Sparkman, 435 U.S. 349 (1978).

Sullivan, T. (1992). *Sexual abuse and the rights of children: Reforming Canadian law.* Toronto: University of Toronto Press.

Thurman, S. K. (Ed.). (1985). *Children of handicapped parents.* New York: Academic Press.

Wickham-Searl, P. (1992). Mothers with a mission. In P. M. Ferguson, D. L. Ferguson, & S. J. Taylor (Eds.), *Interpreting disability: A qualitative reader* (pp. 251–274). New York: Teachers College Press.

Wolfensberger, W. (1972). *The principle of normalization in human services.* Toronto: National Institute on Mental Retardation.

Wood, S. (1988). Parents: Whose partners? In L. Barton (Ed.), *The politics of special education needs* (pp. 190–207). London: Falmer.

Yuker, H. E. (Ed.). (1988). *Attitudes toward persons with disabilities.* New York: Springer.

About the Authors

Ellen Brantlinger's research has focused on the social/sexual development of adolescents with mental retardation and on the care providers' attitudes toward the sexuality of their clients. She is Associate Professor in the Division of Special Education in the Department of Curriculum and Instruction at Indiana University.

Susan Klein's expertise is in the area of parent/professional communication and the roles of parents in service delivery systems. She is Professor of Special Education in the Curriculum and Instruction Department at Indiana University.

Samuel Guskin has a long history of research on attitude development and stereotypes of people with mental retardation. He is Professor of Special Education and Educational Psychology at Indiana University.